CREATING HEAVEN ON EARTH

A CONTEMPORARY INTERPRETATION OF SCRIPTURE

JOY BRISBANE

© Copyright 2024 Joy Brisbane – All rights reserved.

Published in the United States by Hill of Content Publishing

Published in the United Kingdom by Hill of Content Publishing

Published in Australia by Hill of Content Publishing

Published in India by Hill of Content Publishing

Distributed by Etoile International Group. Hong Kong.

hillofcontentpublishing.com

PO Box 24 East Melbourne 8002 Victoria Australia

Cover design: Peta French * *Interior design:* Will Gerard

All rights reserved. No part of this publication may be reproduced, stored in a retrieval system or transmitted in any form by any means without the prior permission of the copyright owner. Enquiries should be made to the publisher. Every effort has been made to ensure that this book is free from error or omissions. However, the Publisher, the Author, the Editor or their respective employees or agents, shall not accept responsibility for injury, loss or damage occasioned to any person acting or refraining from action as a result of material in this book whether or not such injury, loss or damage is in any way due to any negligent act or omission, breach of duty or default on the part of the Publisher, the Author, the Editor, or their respective employees or agents. The Author, the Publisher, the Editor and their respective employees or agents do not accept any responsibility for the actions of any person - actions which are related in any way to information contained in this book.

National Library of Australia Cataloguing-in-Publication data:

Brisbane, Joy,
Creating Heaven on Earth

Includes index: ISBN: 978-0-6483443-3-9

CONTENTS

Foreword	vii
Answering the Call	ix
1. What Is Spirit?	1
2. What Is Righteousness?	3
3. Consider The Lilies	5
4. Judgement	8
5. Openings	11
6. Do Unto Others	15
7. Lifting Of Burdens	18
8. Parables	23
9. Christ Energy	28
10. Soul Profit	35
11. Our Greatness	39
12. The Child	43
13. The Eye Of The Needle	47
14. Of Service	51
15. The Shepherd	55
16. The Need to Be Right	58
17. What is Sin?	63
18. The Temple	67
19. Faith	71
20. The Light	74
21. The Well	77
22. The Dead Shall Hear	81
23. Easter	85
24. Truth	89
25. Gods	94
26. Home of Spirit	98
27. I Am The Way	101
28. Manifestations	105
The Journey	109
Also by Joy Brisbane	117

White Lily
[for my mother]

Softly my heart sings, my mother.
Your presence, your light touches my soul.
A spring breeze sways white blossoms.
And you, my white lily,
You are my spring breeze,
The breath of pure love
Moving my spirit mysteriously.

I see you in my mind.
I hear your voice raised in songs of praise.
Crystal clear notes through the ether
Are the memories of my inner child.
Even then, you were merged with
The brilliance of divine light and
Intimate with the greatness of love.
And still, you and He are one.

In this moment of stillness
The world, with all its worries,
Recedes beyond my awareness.
I come to the garden alone
To find you patiently waiting.

Walk beside me, my mother,
My white lily of purity and peace.
My ragged voice is silent,
But deep within my joyful heart sings.

FOREWORD

REV TIM COSTELLO
President of the Baptist Union of Australia (1999–2002)
CEO of World Vision Australia (2003–2016)

I am not in the habit of recommending books from a medium or psychic, but when that person was raised as a Christian and is negotiating her past, I appreciate the effort and I understand that journey. When that medium is taking the words of Jesus and interpreting their meaning for themselves, I applaud that. I daily meditate on the teachings of Jesus myself. I may disagree with many of the authors interpretations, but I love the authenticity of her project.

The last census showed that nearly a majority of Australians ticked the box - No Religion. But that certainly does not mean no faith. This book speaks to many who ticked that box! And when she says Jesus was not a Christian, I think of one of my heroes, Archbishop Desmond Tutu, writing a book *God is Not a Christian*.

Thank you for your search reflected in this book. A pleasure to read.

ANSWERING THE CALL

Are you seeking healing for grief, for a heart that hurts, and a mind in turmoil? So often we wander through life, struggling to keep going, hungering for answers, when help is all around us... both in spirit and in our human world.

I am not religious. I have no affiliations with any religion. I am deeply spiritual.

I have always struggled with the concept of there being a single entity called God. How can there be such a being who controls all of the universes, the cosmos? For me, the power such a being would hold would be beyond belief or faith. Science is now proving there is more than one universe, and it will take a very long time for them to investigate our own before they even begin on the others. The extent of the cosmos is beyond our ability to comprehend. How can one being have control over the entire cosmos?

However, I do believe in a collective force of many thousands of beings of a highly evolved nature. This realm I call Great Spirit. And I believe we are all a minute part of that magical and magnificent spirit, for it not only exists outside of us, but such energy is contained within our soul-self. That is the best way I can describe something to which none of us truly have the answers. And my assessment comes from working with these realms for almost sixty years, and the study of highly educated and evolved souls, who themselves have written on this subject for centuries.

I am a psychic medium. I embrace the wisdom of all the great masters who have walked this planet and I am privileged to be able to connect with some of these wise beings in spirit.

To me, a master is a highly evolved soul who has earned the right to be called a master and is not gender specific. There have been many such masters going back from modern times to the ancient ones. Each era brings with it such people who are relevant to that time in history; who are teachers and leaders, healers, and philosophers; people who renew ancient wisdom and make it accessible to the seeker adding, as they go, their own particular understanding of such wisdom.

One of these powerful beings made it clear to me that the time has come for me to bring a different point of view to ancient writings based on his life. Known to Christians as Jesus – he is known to me as Yeshua.

My religious background is that of Christianity. My dad was a lay preacher in the Uniting Church, Australia. As a young person I diligently followed where my dad led me. But as adulthood grew within me, so did the ability to think beyond the confines of religious beliefs and restrictions.

I never was one to be told what I should or should not believe. I have always held strongly to my right to understand what is true and real for me, and to allow all people to embrace the belief that they love. I never could understand why people killed for the sake of religion. And I could never accept that Christianity was the only doorway to heaven, or that any of the religions held the secret to ongoing spiritual existence beyond our human self.

I began to explore many beliefs, finally coming to understand that a walk with spirit was an inner journey that needed no adherence to any organised form, or doctrine, of religion. I remember well the day it dawned on me that religion and spirituality were two different things. They can, and often do go together, as my beautiful mother showed me. When I realised I did not need to be religious to be deeply spiritual – that was the day I was set free to follow my own path, allowing it to unfold before me as I walked with spirit.

Back in 2006, after my husband had died, I was sitting quietly alone in my newly built home contemplating my future, when out of the ether came a booming voice that deeply frightened me. This big masculine voice said, "The time is not now!" It was in answer to a question I had been contemplating about stepping into a new way forward. I am someone who has been used to living with esoteric experiences since I was seven years of age but even for me, that voice left me shaken. To this day I can still 'hear' it and get shivers when I think about it.

Years later when Yeshua came through to me in meditation and asked me to return to the Bible and bring to the people a different understanding of what has been written, of what he said, I momentarily froze. And then I cried. I cried tears of pain for a youth that had been filled with fear and judgements, a youth based on rights and wrongs around a man called Jesus, around the idea of hell's fire and damnation, and the belief that the only way to enter the "kingdom of heaven" was through the doctrine of the church.

Images within the memories of my childhood arose from the dark passages of my subconscious mind. A belt being pulled from my dad's trousers as he prepared to discipline me in the ways of righteousness. Long and cold hours spent sitting on uncomfortable seats as some man droned on about the need to repent of my awful sins. Conversations about the heathen religions that created fear in my heart. The flood gates of childhood memories had been opened. I yelled at him, "You have got to be kidding me! No way. No way will I go back to that time!" And then I heard in the Master's strong, commanding, yet tender voice, "Not only will you bring a different way of thinking about the texts within that book, but it will help you to heal that part of your youth. I will be working with you."

Yeshua is unlimited in all that he does. He never was a Christian. Christianity arrived after his death. He was born into a Jewish family. At age twelve he went through the ritual of gaining his bar mitzvah as Jewish boys still do. The Christ energy is not limited to Christians; it belongs to all people. It is an energy – not a person. It is the energy of love and enlightenment. Yeshua embodied the Christ energy as have thousands before him and since his life. He was no ordinary man, but a highly evolved soul, a master, and a prophet who is just as relevant today as he was two thousand years ago.

I have worked with the writings of the four apostles – Matthew, Mark, Luke, and John – in the King James version of the Bible's New Testament.

May the insights I have gained, by revisiting these texts with a different mindset, help you to come into a deeper understanding of self, of the realm of spirit, and to walk the path that is right for you. No glove ever fits all hands. Follow your own heart, your own truth. There is no right or wrong – there is only enlightenment and love.

There have been moments throughout my life where I have experienced such bliss. When it happens, when I feel the extreme love and support that comes from those in spirit toward me, there is nothing more profoundly magical and beautiful. I - am – in - heaven!

1

WHAT IS SPIRIT?

I can only come into heavenly bliss when I am poor in the spirit of ego.

SCRIPTURE

Matthew 5:3

"Blessed are the poor in spirit for theirs is the kingdom of heaven."

The Oxford dictionary says of spirit:

The non-physical part of a person which is the seat of emotions and character – the soul.

It is a hard word to define – spirit. It is by nature unseen and therefore hard to describe.

INTERPRETATION

I have come to believe we have two spirits:

- That of our human Self supported by the ego.
- That of our divine eternal Self encased in our soul.

I have no doubt that the realm of spirit is incredibly vast. That which we call Heaven, I believe to be complex – a place of healing, creativity, learning, and exquisite beauty.

I also believe we do not need to physically die to enter into Heaven.

> When I am in Heaven, I am in bliss.
> When I am in bliss, I am in heaven.

REFLECTION

I do not feel that Yeshua was talking about being poor in our divine spirit. Rather, I feel he was talking about being poor in the spirit of the ego. When the spirit of the ego falls silent and we listen to the voice of our soul's spirit, we come into love and enlightenment… we touch Heaven.

I can only come into heavenly bliss when I am poor in the spirit of ego.

2

WHAT IS RIGHTEOUSNESS?

The journey to become the very best you can be.

SCRIPTURE

Matthew 5:6

"Blessed are they who do hunger and thirst after righteousness, for they will be filled."

Oxford Dictionary:

Righteousness: The quality of being morally right or justifiable.

Similar words – virtue, uprightness, decency, integrity, worthiness, honesty, morality, innocence, justice.

INTERPRETATION

The word righteousness covers many bases. We often hear the statement – she/he is self-righteous; meaning they hold self above others, placing themselves on a pedestal, are judgemental, and see themselves as being more moral and right. The 'Holier than thou' attitude. But that was not what

Yeshua meant when he used that particular word. As we so often do with our English language, we have changed the meaning of the word – this time from something beautiful into something negative.

As I meditated on what he truly meant as righteous, here is what came to me:

Those who work toward releasing all negative thoughts and feelings toward self and others, they open up a space to be filled with self-worth, forgiveness of self and others, higher levels of integrity, honesty, and love. They allow the light of the divine to enter rather than the energy of the ego. In so doing, their lives become more fulfilling, and they know the joy of abundance in all of its forms. They become self-righteous. Put another way – within self all is made right.

REFLECTION

What you believe you create. If you sit in the beliefs of negative, ego-driven thoughts and feelings – that is what you will draw to you. If you allow yourself to "hunger and thirst" after self-worth, integrity, honesty, and love – that is what will naturally flow back to you. And you will feel truly blessed. You will be filled with peace, wonder, and joy.

According to how Yeshua meant it – being self-righteous means working on one's inner journey to become the very best they can be.

3

CONSIDER THE LILIES

Be the beautiful soul you are. It is enough!

SCRIPTURE

Matthew 6: 28 and 29

28. *"Why take ye thought for the raiment? Consider the lilies of the field, how they grow; they toil not, neither do they spin."*

29. *" And yet I say unto you that even Solomon in all his glory was not arrayed like one of these."*

INTERPRETATION

We become so bound up in material possessions, trying to create beauty in our outer world, we fail to see it is the beauty of the inner world that needs to be seen and addressed. So, let us do as the Master suggested, let us consider the lilies of the field…of the field being the clue here.

- They are growing wild and free. There are no

limitations on them, no boundaries set by what others might want of them.
- They don't ask to be accepted, or even recognised for their beauty. They bloom and grow for the sake of doing so.
- Do they get upset if other plants grow with them? No, of course not, they grow in harmony with the other plants of the field.
- When hardships come, as they do during drought times, do they cry out against such hardships? No, they simply go into dormancy, and there they wait in stillness until the abundance of rain comes again. Then they are reborn.
- As their flowers begin to wilt and die off, do they struggle against the cycle? No, they understand that they have to let go of the old blooms to make way for the new ones. They let go of that which no longer serves them. They also understand that, in letting go of the old blooms, those blooms of the past create the fertile ground for the new of the future.

King Solomon's palace was spared no money in the creation of that magnificent dwelling. It was glorified with gold, beautiful handmade tiles, silk adornments, handmade carpets of the finest quality, and gems of many kinds. Yet for all of his efforts, he never found the exquisite beauty that comes with simplicity, contentment, self-love, and by being true to self – as the lilies did.

REFLECTION

There is a sense to these verses, a message to take time out to be in nature, to see that which we take so much for granted, to see the beauty all around us, connecting to the energy of Mother Earth. To understand that no matter what garments we wear, what makeup we put on our faces, what exercises we might do to look gorgeous, true beauty comes from within our positive thoughts and feelings, and through our ability to love the self and others.

True beauty is not the gilding of Solomon's palace, not the garments we place on our bodies, but is in the purity and innocence of the lily that blossoms for the joy of being what it is. Be the beautiful soul you are. It is enough!

4

JUDGEMENT

What flows out from you comes back to you – every time!

SCRIPTURE

Matthew 7:1 and 2

1. *"Judge not that ye be not judged."*

2. *"For with what judgement ye judge, ye shall be judged; and with what measure you mete, it shall be measured to you again."*

INTERPRETATION

All aspects of our existence are based on both a circle and a cycle. Earth turns. The seasons go through their cycles. We are born, grow, age, then die to return to spirit to move through the process all over again that we might, at a soul level, grow, expand, become enlightened, and move toward our greatness. The entire cosmos is based on circles and cycles. Have the scientists ever discovered a square planet? Day moves to night, night back into day.

So it is with what we put out from our minds and hearts. What you give out comes back to you. That is the simple message the Master was teaching – if you judge another, they will immediately return the judgement.

If I were to say to you, "I don't like you." How would you react? Perhaps with an equal energy, "Yeah, well you are not so great yourself." Or words to that effect. But how would you reply if I were to say to you, "You have a gorgeous smile and a kind heart." You might say something like, "Thank you. You are also a nice person."

The difference between judgement and assessment:

- Judgement becomes a statement of fact. This person is good, this person is bad.
- Assessment is an analysis toward potentially creating something better. This is not a good situation – how can I help change it. This person is brilliant with their gift – something great can come of this.

This return of judgement not only applies to our reaction to others, it can also apply to Self.

- I am a bad driver. You will always be a bad driver until you believe you can do better, because what you put out, what you think and believe, you create.
- No one ever understands me. And no person ever will if that is what you believe.
- I can't get my head around this problem. You had better take a deep breath and change the way you are thinking. Every problem has a solution.
- So and so doesn't love me. It is hard to love someone who believes you don't love them.
- There is no end to this hardship. Ooh, you had better flip that coin from tails up to heads up. Take a look at

the people competing in the Para-Olympics. I wonder how they got to be Olympians? Perhaps they flipped the coin and told themselves they would never allow their disability to defeat them.
- Being poor is being spiritual. Okay, if you want to continue to struggle all your life, you keep on thinking that. Spirituality is an inner journey with your mind, heart, and soul, not an outer journey with finances. I know poor people who are deeply spiritual. I also know wealthy people who are deeply spiritual and use their wealth to help improve others situations. Poverty and spirituality do not go hand in hand. It is a choice one makes and there is no right or wrong to it. That choice is a karmic journey with Self.

REFLECTION

When we change our negative thinking or feeling toward another, and toward Self, then a new circle is created.

What measure you mete; it shall be measured to you again. What flows out from you comes back to you – every time!

5

OPENINGS

*Open the door and welcome home your
true Self, your own divinity.*

SCRIPTURE

Matthew 7: 7 and 8

7. *"Ask and it shall be given you; seek and ye shall find; knock and it shall be opened unto you."*

8. *"For everyone that asketh receiveth; and he that seeketh findeth; and to him that knocketh it shall be opened."*

INTERPRETATION

Let us take each of these sayings of the Master in turn, but before doing so, I wish to say I do not believe that Yeshua was talking about our outer world. Rather, I am being directed to write about our inner world. Having said that, I believe it also applies to our outer world when we are in a place of faith, integrity, and grace. When we are connected to our wonderful spirit guides, there is no end to what we can manifest in our lives – providing we are coming from desires that are based in truth and are for the greater good of all. There are many examples of how this has worked, but it takes trust in our own soul and in our spirit beings, working together to create such outcomes.

"Ask and it shall be given you – for everyone that asketh receiveth."

- Are you seeking help in some way for a resolution to a situation?
- Do you need direction in life?
- Is peace, love, and happiness what your heart craves?
- Do you want to expand beyond who you perceive yourself to be? To get out of ruts in which you feel trapped?
- Are you seeking healing for grief, for a heart that hurts, and a mind in turmoil?

So often we wander through life, struggling to keep going, hungering for answers, when help is all around us... both in spirit and in our human world.

Our spirit guides can do little until we ask. We were born with a thing called free will, and not even the greatest of the masters or angels can interfere in our free will. Can you imagine their sense of frustration, when they are waiting for us to ask for help, and we keep on struggling in our limited human Self? Their help comes in many different ways:

- Messages in dreams
- A book that jumps out at you
- A person that just happens to enter your life
- Clarity of thought and feeling – intuition
- Words in a newspaper, program on television, words of a song

To name a few. The secret in obtaining help from the realm of spirit is in not telling them their job. When we want something in a particular way, then we block all other avenues through which help can come. The secret is in asking specifically what it is you need, then let go and allow spirit to work their miracles. They have the big picture that we don't have. When we place conditions on the asking, then we limit the possibilities through which that help can come. It may not come in the way or the timing we want it – but it will come.

"Seek and ye shall find… and he that seeketh findeth."

We have all lived through centuries of lifetimes – here on planet Earth and elsewhere in the cosmos. With each incarnation we gather into our soul's memory bank wisdom and knowledge, gained through our perceived negative and positive experiences. [Often that which appears negative is in truth a blessing that will lead us to a greater understanding of our deeper journey with Self.]

When we go deeper into self through meditation, prayer, teachings, workshops, study, listening through music, or any other way that fits for us as individuals – seeking to find our true Self, seeking the wisdom and knowledge stored in that amazing computer in our brain, that part called the subconscious – then through the stillness will come the answers.

Likewise, when we go on a quest to find out who is with us in spirit – they will come to us. Again, let go of the how and when. They are already with us and have been from the moment of conception within our mother's womb. Be willing and open to any way in which they may present themselves – through a medium, a dream, a vision, or just a knowingness – and remove from thoughts and feelings the 'I am not worthy'. Nothing will block a guide from coming through to you quicker than 'I am not worthy'. Our beings in spirit live with pure truth. When we say, 'I am not worthy', our guides will back off and wait until we believe we are worthy of their presence.

When we actively seek answers, fulfillment, truth, understanding, peace, and love – they will come to us in the exact right moment.

"Knock and it shall be opened unto you – and to him that knocketh it shall be opened."

When you both ask and seek, you are in fact knocking on spirits door – both your own inner divine door to the spirit of your soul, and the door to the realm of spirit. And both will open that door and welcome you home to your true Self, to your own divinity and to the collective wisdom, knowledge, and love within Self, and within the realm of spirit.

The only person who can close that door is our human Self. Once open, neither the realm of spirit nor our own soul can close that door. Another way of putting it: when we leave the safety of our garden, unlocking the gate to the fields beyond and set ourselves free to go on a journey, a quest of spiritual enlightenment, then the gate remains open – unless – we return to the safety of the garden again [our human Self] and close the gate on our spiritual advancement.

REFLECTION

The choice is always ours – to knock on the door to enlightenment, or keep it firmly closed. But if you knock – spirit will answer and open the door to a new way of being and doing.

When you ask and seek – you knock.

6

DO UNTO OTHERS

What you give out comes back to you.

SCRIPTURE

Matthew 7:12

"Therefore all things whatsoever ye would that men should do unto you, do ye even so unto them: For this is the law and the prophet."

INTERPRETATION

The first part of this quote from Yeshua has a similar base to its action as my previous writing about judgement. What you do to others is what they will do in return. If you want to be respected, loved, valued, and accepted for who you are – then that is what you need to give out to others. Remember - what you give out comes back to you.

- Positive actions create positive results
- Negative actions create negative results

It is that simple – and that difficult. It is perhaps the second biggest lesson for us to learn as Human Beings... the biggest lesson is that of learning to love unconditionally both Self and others. In learning this lesson of 'doing unto others how we want to be treated' we prepare the way to learn to love without condition.

But the second part of what Yeshua said – *For this is the law and the prophet* – now that is a whole new ball game.

"For this is the law":

I believe the 'law' that Yeshua was speaking about here was neither a law of the government nor a law of religion. He was speaking about a universal law – the law of attraction. As I have written before:

- What you believe – you create
- What you give out comes back to you

It is a never-ending circle and cycle. It is the infinite law of the universe. And we can change our world by shifting our thinking, creating a more positive way of living, and seeking help to heal at all levels.

"And the prophet":

From the Oxford Dictionary:

- *In the Christian, Jewish, and Muslim religions a person sent by God to teach the people and give them messages from God*
- *A person who claims to know what will happen in the future*
- *A person who teaches or supports a new idea, theory*

In other words - *For this is the law and the prophet* – this is the universal law, the message from spirit as taught to us by those who are the voice of Great Spirit, [Yeshua being one of those prophets], this is the new way forward. To create harmony on this planet we need to do unto others as we would have them do unto us.

The ultimate goal could be to love all of mankind unconditionally. Will we ever get to that place? I don't know – but I can have a lot of fun, and grow within myself a great deal, by giving it a go!

REFLECTION

As with the majority of 'so-called' New Age ways of being – this ancient message is perhaps more relevant today than it ever has been. As the teachings of Yeshua show, there is very little that is new in this age of Aquarius.

7

LIFTING OF BURDENS

Finding peace and rest in our heart and soul.

SCRIPTURE

Matthew 11:28 to 30

28. *"Come unto me all ye that labour and are heavy laden, and I will give you rest."*

29. *"Take my yoke upon you, and learn of me: For I am meek and lowly of heart: And ye shall find rest unto your souls."*

30. *"For my yoke is easy and my burden is light."*

INTERPRETATION

So what exactly is a yoke?

A yoke is a wooden beam normally used between a pair of oxen or other animals to enable them to pull together on a load when working in pairs, as oxen usually do; some yokes are fitted to individual animals. There are several types of yokes, used in different cultures, and for different types of oxen. A pair of oxen may be called a yoke of oxen, and yoke is also a verb, as in "to yoke a pair of oxen". Other animals that may be yoked include horses, mules, donkeys, and water buffalo.

From the Oxford dictionary:

To join two animals together with a yoke; to attach an animal to something with a yoke

- *(be) yoked together* - A pair of oxen, yoked together, was used
- *(be) yoked to something* - an ox yoked to a plough
- *(formal) to bring two people, countries, ideas, etc. together so that they are forced into a close relationship*

Yeshua was great at getting messages over through imagery and symbolism, and these three verses are typical of his use of visualisations. Where he says, take my yoke upon you, he does not mean in a literal way to physically carry his yoke.

"Come unto me all ye that labour and are heavy laden, and I will give you rest."

When these words were spoken Yeshua was in physical form. Remembering that he was a teacher and a prophet, the voice of Great Spirit, then a different way of saying this would be:

Come and sit with me all you people who are heavy of heart, who carry burdens that are weighing you down, and I will teach you how to let go of that which is worrying you. I will share with you my wisdom and knowledge so you may come into a place of peace and rest.

Even though he is no longer in physical form, the same is as true and real today as it was then. For two thousand years people have been seeking his spirit presence in their lives. It is the mark of a true master that, after such a huge amount of time, the inhabitants of this planet are still seeking out his wisdom and help. The same can be said of the Buddha and many other great masters.

How can we hear his teachings and absorb his wisdom when Yeshua is no longer in physical form? Unless you are fortunate to be able to use your psychic gifts, then the connection to his spirit requires a lot of trust and an inner hunger to know more, BE more, and to find that deep peace that simply IS. It requires being in stillness through meditation or prayer. He has a different way of speaking to us now through:

- Our intuition
- A song
- Books such as this one and films
- Words another person has spoken
- Workshops
- Dreams and visions

Our masters in spirit are unlimited in ways to connect with us. Yeshua will use any way that is available to him to make that connection. However, remember, we have free will. Unless we are willing to be open to such a connection, to come into his presence and sit with him, then he can yell as loud as he likes, and we still won't hear what he is saying to us.

"Take my yoke upon you, and learn of me:"

Remember the definition? *A yoke is a wooden beam normally used between a pair of oxen or other animals to enable them to pull together.* Simply he is saying connect with me, walk beside me, let us pull together to help you achieve what you need, and I will teach you how to be at peace and to come into a deeper understanding of your Self. Learn from my example [*learn of me*].

"*For I am meek and lowly of heart: And ye shall find rest unto your souls.*"

I am meek and lowly of heart – I am at peace within myself, without tension.

- Meek – without anger or resentment, without needing the attention and admiration of others
- Lowly of heart – without the egos need for a grandiose way of being

When the mind rules our lives and the ego dominates, we become separated from the beauty, energy, and voice of our soul. We find peace and rest in our heart and soul when we let go of the negative aspects of our journey with our Human Self, and when we no longer need to feel bigger and better than others. Yeshua was saying - this is where I have got to, and I want to help you get to that place within your own inner journey.

"*For my yoke is easy and my burden is light.*"

Simply - it is easy to connect with him [yoke], and he won't create a difficult way forward for us. We are the ones that create the burden in our minds and hearts. We are the ones that block our way forward through fear. It is us who become stubborn, trying to do everything from the energy of thought rather than allowing things to unfold naturally and quietly. It is easy to blame those in spirit for the toughness of our journeys, but they are never to blame. We create our outcomes through our thoughts and desires. If those thoughts and desires are positive, then we will create magic in our lives. If they are negative, then our way forward will be difficult.

REFLECTION

The masters will do everything they can to help us, but they cannot do it for us. Yeshua cannot interfere in our free will.

8

PARABLES

It all begins with self-forgiveness and deep honesty.

SCRIPTURE

Matthew 13: 3 to 9

1. "*And he spake many things to them in parables, saying, Behold, a sower went forth to sow.*"

2. "*And when he sowed, some seeds fell by the wayside, and the fowls came and devoured them up.*"

3. "*Some fell upon stony places, where they had not much earth: and forthwith they sprung up, because they had no deepness of earth.*"

4. "*And when the sun was up, they were scorched; and because they had no root, they were withered away.*"

5. "*Some fell upon stoney places, where they had not much earth: and forthwith they sprung up, because they had no deepness of earth.*"

6. *"And when the sun was up, they were scorched, and because they had no root, they withered away."*

7. *"And some fell among thorns; and the thorns sprung up, and choked them."*

8. *"But other fell into good ground, and brought forth fruit, some an hundredfold, some sixtyfold, some thirtyfold."*

9. *"Who hath ears to hear, let him hear."*

INTERPETATION

Yeshua used imagery and symbolism in the form of parables. A parable is a story used to get a message across, either of a moral or spiritual kind. Sometimes the story relates both to morality and spirituality as does the parable of the 'sower'. The message in this story relates both to our involvement with the outer world and to the journey with inner growth and understanding.

The Outer World:

Sharing who we are, our wisdom, knowledge gained from our experiences, and our gifts – as much as we may want to 'save' the whole world and enlighten people – we will only touch those who are ready to be touched. And there are times when the seeds we wish to sow are not what the other may want or need.

In our garden of life, some people prefer roses to daisies. There is no right or wrong to another's journey in life, there are only choices. We may not agree with or like those choices, but that does not make those choices wrong. We never know what karmic journey others are on, what laws of balance from previous lifetimes are being played out, what a soul has put their hand up to experience so they may advance in their growth. Nor do we know what role an individual has chosen to play so that others may learn how to be strong, to have courage, and learn to stand in their own power. I often use the example of the bully in the workplace teaching others to find their voice and learn to stand up for who they are. Those being bullied are there to teach the bully how to do things differently, in a more gentle and caring way.

There are many paths that lead to the top of the same mountain. Some folks wish to walk slowly and absorb the intricate growth as they take each step. Some folks like to jog to get there quicker so they may scan the horizon. Others prefer to climb the cliff face, exerting a great amount of energy, feeling the excitement of achievement. Some may take many lifetimes to learn the same lesson, whilst others will grab its meaning quickly. Does it matter? After all, the soul is eternal and therefore has all of eternity to grow and expand into its greatness.

If you are someone who is actively working in the world to help people to heal; someone who is dedicated to bringing peace and enlightenment to others; remember - not everyone will want to participate, or are ready for that which you wish to share. Growth of any kind cannot be forced. It is not for us to try and push someone else into our beliefs. It is our place to gently guide them into a deeper awareness of their own truth.

There is a saying: When the student is ready the teacher will come. I believe the opposite is also true. When the teacher reaches a certain level of expertise, the students at that level will come. The teacher is also the student, and the student the teacher. Don't try to sow your seeds where the resistance of solid rock is present, for there will be no growth and your efforts will be lost. Learn where your rightful place is meant to be, then sow your seeds in fertile ground. This applies to all areas of life – work, relationships, and your own inner growth.

The Inner World:

Our outer world reflects our inner world. Our inner world reflects our outer world. As within, so without. As without, so within.

If within our inner world we carry the seeds of anger, hatred, disrespect, and judgement, you can be guaranteed that is what you will sow in your outer world. That is a tough and uncomfortable place to be. They are the seeds of the thorns that choke the healthy growth of self-love and love for others. Like the seeds that fell on poor soil, the growth will be minimal and without strength. What you sow you reap. And what you reap are the seeds that you will then sow again.

How do we create the fertile ground, within our hearts and minds, so we may sow the seeds that lead to inner growth? It all begins with self-forgiveness and deep honesty. Self-judgement and recrimination only serve to push us into depression, anxiety, and feelings of worthlessness. Nothing beautiful or nourishing can grow in such poisoned soil. Seek to release all trauma from the past. Deliberately and consciously feed the soil within your mind and heart with the goodness that will allow the beautiful seeds that land there the ability to increase a *hundredfold* - a hundred percent growth.

How does one begin to prepare the soil within our hearts and minds?

- Seek out counselling to release the effects of negative experiences
- Begin to meditate and join a meditation group
- Read books on personal growth and spirituality
- Listen to podcasts on such subjects
- Take note every time you say something negative

about yourself and shift that thought to a more positive one
- Write in a journal. As you move forward in your personal growth, it is good to look back at how far you have come. And often we write little gems of which we need to be reminded

REFLECTION

Ultimately, we are the ones who allow the planting of the seeds of thorns that choke us, or the seeds that nourish our minds and hearts. Shift your consciousness onto a path that will gently and deliberately take you up the mountain to self-attainment, self-love, and finally - enlightenment.

Who hath ears to hear, let him hear.

CHRIST ENERGY

We are never alone. We all have loved ones in spirit.

SCRIPTURE

Matthew 16: 13 to 19

13. "When Jesus came into the coasts of Caesarea Philippi, he asked his disciples, saying, Whom do men say that I the Son of man am?"

14. "And they said, Some say thou art John the Baptist: some Elias; and others, Jeremias, or one of the prophets."

15. "He saith unto them, But whom say ye that I am?"

16. "And Simon Peter answered and said, Thou art the Christ, the Son of the living God."

17. "And Jesus answered and said unto him, Blessed art thou, Simon Barjona: for flesh and blood hath not revealed it unto thee, but my Father which is in Heaven."

18. "And I say unto thee, That though art Peter, and upon this rock I will build my church; and the gates of hell shall not prevail against it."

19. *"And I will give unto thee the keys of the kingdom of heaven; and whatsoever thou shalt bind on earth shall be bound in heaven."*

INTERPRETATION

This piece of writing is loaded with many messages. I will take some of these verses to explore more fully what was being said. But before I do, there are some differences here between what I believe and what many Christians believe. I can only interpret from my place of truth, and what I believe I am being guided to say by Yeshua. I leave it up to you, to decide what is right for you. Here are the differences:

- Son of man – that is to say, don't forget I am also a human being.
- Thou art the Christ – a man who has embodied the Christ energy.
- Son of the living God. Is God a single being or a living, breathing, magnificent energy that is the culmination of all of spirit. For me personally, Great Spirit is how I see God.
- Heaven - both a place in spirit and what we create within our mind, heart, and soul.
- Hell – what we create in our minds and hearts and not a place where we are sent beyond death. I do not believe in an eternal place of torment and torture. That is not to say that within our cosmos there are no hellish places according to our understanding of the word. Planet Mars could be one such place. Our souls incarnate over and over again in order to grow and expand into their greatness. Why would we be prevented from learning and growing by being condemned in such a way?
- Church - is commonly known as a physical place of worship within the Christian faith. But the origin of

the word church comes from the Greek word
Ekklesia (or ecclesia) meaning a gathering of people.

"Whom do men say that I - the Son of man - am?"

I often feel we do Yeshua a disservice not acknowledging his human journey – *Son of man*. We are so ready to put him on a pedestal as heir to the throne of David, for the prophet that he was, and for his divinity. But Yeshua was also a man, and these few words say it all. He knew fully that he was walking a tight rope with both the Roman authorities and those of his own people. Yeshua was a rebel who was dissatisfied with the authoritarian nature of Jewish law, and he turned everything upside down to make people think beyond what they were told they must believe.

Every now and then I get a tiny insight into what he went through as he brought to the people a new and more modern way of thinking and believing. This was a man who had disappeared off the scene for twenty plus years. During that time he travelled to many lands and had his eyes opened to different ways of living, and to different spiritual practices outside of his Jewish laws and those of the Romans. He had learned new ways of healing, gathered information both of a historical and spiritual nature, and had been a student to learned people from many other cultures. Yeshua was a man of the world. The confines of Jewish law at that time were not for him.

Yeshua was charismatic. He drew people to him. And, as with all ages, there were those who were ready for change; ready to walk a different path. But he also knew the risk he was taking to kick against the laws of that time. Here, in this question - *Whom do men say that I ... am?* – we find the human Yeshua curios, perhaps a little afraid, but definitely beginning to prepare himself for a future he probably knew he was walking into. He knew the old ways would not be let go of easily, and some people would see him as a traitor to his heritage as heir to the throne of David, and to Jewish law.

"He saith unto them, But whom say ye that I am? And Simon Peter answered and said, Thou art the Christ, the Son of the living God."

It is my understanding that the Christ is not a singular person but an energy. The Christ energy for me is that of unconditional love, self-empowerment for the greater good of all, enlightenment, understanding within both the intellect and the heart, compassion, wisdom, and an all-encompassing desire to reach out to others. We can all embody the Christ energy as he did. It is not exclusive to one man. There are other references within the New Testament of Yeshua allowing his disciples to realise that they too could embody the Christ energy. Referring to everything that he had done in his short time on the planet he told them – this you will also do and more! And we continue to do so.

Yeshua was testing his disciples to see if they understood what he was trying to bring to the people. *But whom say ye that I am?* Peter's answer – *"Thou art the Christ, the Son of the living God"* – allowed Yeshua to see that Peter had grabbed the concept of what the prophet was trying to convey to them. Son of the living God for me means a soul that is one with and a part of Great Spirit... born/created from that energy of unconditional love – as we all are. When we come into our Human Self as a baby, we come with free will – to learn more and to become more aligned with the Christ energy, or to go down the path of negative feelings and thoughts.

This was a whole new way forward for his disciples; to become subservient to the Jewish and Roman laws, or to find their own truth and embrace the Christ energy. Over two thousand years later, the same choices are still being made.

> "And Jesus answered and said unto him, Blessed art thou, Simon Barjona: for flesh and blood hath not revealed it unto thee, but my Father which is in Heaven."

The meaning of Barjona is most frequently referenced as:

Bar – son of; Jona – the name of Peter's father. Jona I feel would be pronounced Yona. So, Barjona was his sires name – surname. Jona means dove. I also looked up the meaning of Simon - listening, it is heard. Simon [one who listens] Bar [son of] Jona [dove].

It is the only time in the New Testament that Yeshua referred to Peter [Simon Peter Barjona] by his heritage. And I don't feel that was coincidental. I believe it was a deliberate act on Yeshua's behalf to remind Peter of the importance of being a dove – bringing hope and love to the world. I think it was also deliberate of Yeshua to refer to that disciple as Simon rather than his more common name of Peter... you have listened and heard well.

For flesh and blood hath not revealed it unto thee, but my Father which is in Heaven. A different way of saying this statement of Yeshua's would be, your understanding has not come from your human self, but you have heard the voice of my Father who is in spirit. *Father* here does not necessarily translate into God. Yeshua may have been referring to his father, Joseph, who was with him in spirit, and who was working with Peter to help him understand what the Master was trying to convey.

We too have loved ones in spirit, and our guides [one of whom may be Yeshua] who are working day and night to help us overcome problems and to embrace a new way forward. As a psychic medium I encounter such beings on a daily basis.

"And I say unto thee, That though art Peter, and upon this rock I will build my church; and the gates of hell shall not prevail against it."

Simply: The name Peter means rock. Church means a gathering of people. Hell being negative thoughts, feelings, and actions. In other words – Peter was to become the rock, the cornerstone on which gatherings of people would lean upon as they embraced a new way forward; and no amount of negative action on behalf of others would stop the new way from opening up.

Since the horror of the Second World War we are seeing a resurgence in a new way forward, commonly known as The New Age. There is nothing 'new' about The New Age, it is as ancient as Yeshua and way beyond him into BC with other masters' such as the Buddha. We are completing a two-thousand-year cycle from Yeshua's time – the Age of Pisces - as we step into the new Age of Aquarius. It is interesting that Yeshua began his passion and drive for change at the beginning of the Age of Pisces. Each of the astrological ages are approximately two thousand years in length. And, as I write this book, I am deeply touched by, and aware of the significance that it is being written as the new age of Aquarius opens its doors to us. The ancient messages are coming back full cycle, to present themselves in a different way, as we move into the next two thousand years.

"And I will give unto thee the keys of the kingdom of heaven; and whatsoever thou shalt bind on earth shall be bound in heaven."

Remembering that heaven is both a place in spirit and a place we create within our minds and hearts; and the two are closely aligned. As above, so below; as below, so above. What you create within your heart and mind also has its effects within heaven – IF - you care to use the keys that open the way to creating heaven within you. Those keys are held within the Christ energy:

- Unconditional love
- Self-empowerment for the greater good of all
- Enlightenment
- Understanding within both the intellect and the heart
- Compassion
- Wisdom
- All-encompassing desire to reach out to others

REFLECTION

Through our free will we have the choice to embody the Christ energy, or to live with the hell of negative thoughts, feelings, and actions. We always have the choice.

SOUL PROFIT

The greatest treasure we have is the beauty within our own soul.

SCRIPTURE

Matthew 16: 24 to 26

24. "*Then said Jesus unto his disciples, if any man will come after me, let him deny himself, and take up his cross, and follow me.*"

25. "*For whosoever will save his life shall lose it; and whosoever will lose his life for my sake shall find it.*"

26. "*For what is a man profited, if he should gain the whole world and lose his own soul? Or what shall a man give in exchange for his soul?*"

INTERPRETATION

"*If any man come after me*":

In what sense does the Master mean 'come after me'? Does he mean to follow behind him in a physical sense, or is he meaning those who will carry on his work after he has died? Perhaps both are true. Yeshua's use of words, his ability to get messages across to the disciples and the crowds that followed him, they were well chosen and clever. Remember, at this time the disciples were unaware of what Yeshua would have to experience, but he knew. Somewhere inside of him, the prophet knew the authorities would condemn him and crucify him. Again he was subtly preparing his disciples for the final outcome of his radical behaviour.

"let him deny himself, and take up his cross, and follow me."

We need to remember that these words were spoken two thousand years ago, and the exact meaning of that time may differ from our understanding in this age. However, when we look at the meanings of the word deny, we begin to see perhaps a different interpretation to that which my dad and others may have preached. Those words for my dad meant to deny one's importance, to deny ones worth, to be humbled.

My feelings about this verse are dual.

Firstly: If the Master was talking about the physical following of himself – then I believe he was offered as a warning. If you wish to follow me, then you too will have to deny yourselves a long life, because you too will have to carry a cross to the hill of Calvary [where he was crucified]. If this is what you want, then follow me. Crucifixion at that time was the normal punishment for the worst of offenders.

Let us not forget that after these words were spoken, Peter – the rock on which people would rely – denied his association with the heir to the throne of David three times when questioned by the Roman authorities and Jewish leaders just before Yeshua's crucifixion. So if the disciples were to follow him fully to the end, then they would have to deny their right to life.

Secondly: If the Master meant the message for those who would carry on his work beyond his death, his work of healing and helping people to find their own truth within their spiritual journey, then they would have to deny their past, let go of the old ways, and begin a new journey that would probably turn people against them. They would become outcasts from normal society and from their Jewish connections, and that would be their sacrifice, their cross to bear. No doubt at the time Yeshua spoke those words, their full significance would have been lost to the disciples.

"For whosoever will save his life shall lose it; and whosoever will lose his life for my sake shall find it."

At first glance these, words almost seem like a conundrum. Just exactly what did Yeshua mean by this? *Whosoever will save his life shall lose it.* When you relate that sentence to the word deny, another way of saying this could be:

When we concentrate on our physical welfare and survival, and place our greater importance on material wealth and success, then we take ourselves away from our true essence. We are denying the greatness within our soul. We may gain much within our physical world, but run the risk of losing out on true happiness which comes from within, from our deep connection to spirit.

"And whosoever will lose his life for my sake shall find it. "

If you take on board what Yeshua, is saying, then you will go deeper into yourself and find your truth, find what is right for you and not what others demand of you. You will discover the joy of connecting into your soul-self. By letting go of the concentration on, and accumulation of material possessions, hoping they will make you happy, and move to the deeper level of your journey with spirit, then you will find your true Self.

> "For what is a man profited, if he should gain the whole world and lose his own soul? Or what shall a man give in exchange for his soul?"

How many times have we seen people driven by the need for material possessions, for the accumulation of wealth, and still they are miserable? They are continuously trying to fill the emptiness they feel inside.

I do not believe that Yeshua was for one minute suggesting that you need to live in material poverty to be spiritually wealthy. There are wonderful people who have been able to achieve both. Such people often become generous givers to those in need, and powerful leaders in bringing spiritual and inner growth to the world. What he was trying to convey to his disciples was this – there is no material substitute for the discovery of one's inner wealth, the journey of the soul toward sublime happiness.

REFLECTION

When we deny our inner journey, our growth and healing, our awakening to our true Self, no amount of money and material possession can make us happy. The greatest treasure we have is the beauty within our own soul, and nothing can be exchanged for that.

11

OUR GREATNESS

Our souls hold the greatness of our divine spirit.

SCRIPTURE

Matthew 17: 20

"And Jesus said unto them, Because of your unbelief: for verily I say unto you, If ye have the faith as a grain of mustard seed, ye shall say unto this mountain, Remove hence to yonder place; and it shall remove; and nothing shall be impossible unto you."

This message from Yeshua came after he had helped a boy with mental illness to heal. His disciples had been trying to do such healings but without success. They questioned him as to why he could do it and they were unable to do so.

INTERPRETATION

"Because of your unbelief:" Disbelief in our divinity, in the power of our soul, in the ability of the spirit within our soul to heal both self and others, at all levels – physically, mentally, and emotionally – is a huge roadblock to understanding and

working with our full potential. Our souls hold the greatness of our divine spirit.

As I have mentioned in the chapter on *What Is Spirit*; I am aware of having not one but two spirits. The spirit of my soul, and the spirit of my human Self as ruled by the ego. You may have heard the saying, his spirit was broken. In other words, his self-worth was so low that he had no further drive to step up and be himself. He had become subservient. This usually happens when the spirit of the ego has been crushed to such an extent by cruel words and actions, it can no longer cope with life.

The greatness of which I am speaking, and to what Yeshua was referring, was not the spirit of the ego, but the power and magnificence of the soul's spirit. They are two very different spirits.

"If ye have the faith as a grain of mustard seed, ye shall say unto this mountain, Remove hence to yonder place; and it shall remove; and nothing shall be impossible unto you."

What does 'faith' actually mean? Words like assuredness, belief, conviction, and acceptance in something, Self, or someone come to mind.

Again Yeshua was using symbology to get a point across. He was not actually asking the disciples to move physical mountains. What he was referring to were the mountains we create within us, that we feel have become unmovable and insurmountable. The mountains of fear, grief, anger, hatred, lack of self-worth or any other negative thoughts and feelings we have within us; the mountains of illness; the mountains of physical, mental, emotional, and spiritual poverty.

"If ye have the faith as a grain of mustard seed." A mustard seed is tiny. If you had the tiniest bit of faith in the power and energy

of your soul's spirit, you could create miracles. Imagine what it would be like if you could fully trust in the power of your divine spirit, if perhaps you had the faith of an avocado seed! We are great beyond our imagination. The potential within us is massive. Most of us never utilise our full potential. We would likely be a little overwhelmed if we were able to kick start such power hidden within us. And it is an easy switch, a fine line between our ability to stand in the power of our divine spirit and to flip over into the power of the ego. The power of ego says – look at me, I am great, and you are less than me. The power of our divinity says nothing – it simply IS!

"And nothing shall be impossible unto you." Throughout my life as a trained counsellor and psychic medium, I have seen the truth in these words. Through the combined training in counselling with the openness to being a channel for spirit, I have encountered many such miracles as I worked with people. The miracles were not always big, but they were always significant. My mother used to say, "There is no such word as 'can't' dear. All things are possible. There is only 'can't' if that is what is in your mind." And my mother was absolutely correct.

How does one tap into the power of the soul spirit rather than the power of the ego spirit? Here are some guidelines to get you started:

- Meditate/pray to clear your mind and heart of any doubts and lack of self-worth; to become centred in your divinity; and to learn to let go of the influence of the ego.
- Train in some form of hands-on healing modality. Even if you never use it again, it teaches you how to connect into the energy of Great Spirit.
- Train in some form of psychic ability. Again, if you

only use it for yourself, it teaches you how to open up to the bigger energy of Great Spirit.
- Remember it is not you, the human Self, that is doing the work, but your soul-self, the divine aspect of you. The moment you step back into the spirit of the ego, you will lose it.
- Develop, to a deeper level, compassion and understanding for others.
- Find what is true and real for you through reading, doing workshops, and going on a journey of self-discovery.

REFLECTION

We have the power within our divine self, within the Christ energy, to be unlimited in what we can do. We are the great creators of our own lives. Within the physical world we create what we believe we are worth; and we have the potential to bring into our lives, abundance in all of its forms. Within our mental and emotional lives we have the power to heal and to recreate ourselves. Within our spiritual soul-selves we already have the greatness waiting for us to discover our true essence - our divinity.

And what does it take to do all of this?

"If ye have the faith as a grain of mustard seed, ye shall say unto this mountain, Remove hence to yonder place; and it shall remove; and nothing shall be impossible unto you."

12

THE CHILD

Embrace the innocent child within you, and step into the greatness of the energy within your soul.

SCRIPTURE

Matthew 18: 1 to 4

1. "At the same time came the disciples unto Jesus, saying, Who is the greatest in the kingdom of heaven?"

2. "And Jesus called a little child unto him, and set him in the midst of them."

3. "And said, Verily I say unto you, Except ye be converted, and become as little children, ye shall not enter into the kingdom of heaven."

4. "Whosoever therefore shall humble himself as this little child, the same is greatest in the kingdom of heaven."

INTERPRETATION

Remembering that entering into the kingdom of heaven is both a place within Self and a place within spirit, we can begin to see a different way of understanding what Yeshua meant in this example of the child.

Let us take a look at the qualities of a child and see why Yeshua used this child as an example.

- Trust
- Openness
- Vulnerability
- Innocence
- Simple acceptance
- Lives for the moment without concern for tomorrow or hanging on to the past
- Exploration and creativeness
- Allow themselves to be guided by those with greater experience
- Playfulness and spontaneity
- Learns to stand on their own feet, walk, then to run

"Verily I say unto you, Except ye be converted, and become as little children":

Yeshua was not talking about conversion to a religion. After all, he was a Jew, and for Jewish people their religion and way of life is inherited. The conversion he was talking about here is an inner conversion. Perhaps a different way of saying this is – awakening to our inner journey and transformation from who we are, to who we are becoming. The conversion from the negative, ego-driven Self to a being who stands in the purity of child-like qualities.

"Ye shall not enter into the kingdom of heaven."

The kingdom of heaven being a state of bliss, of happiness and peace. Yeshua was not saying, you won't be permitted entry into Heaven beyond death unless you become a child again. He was saying, you won't know the joy of unconditional love, the beauty of living in a state of peace and happiness, unless you let go of all the adult, ego-driven qualities that bring about anger, hatred, discontent, greed, lack of worthiness, and mistrust in self and the world. *'Ye shall not enter'* – does not mean I will stop you, or God will stop you. It means, you will stop yourself from entering into a place or state of bliss by not adopting child-like qualities.

"Whosoever therefore shall humble himself as this little child, the same is greatest in the kingdom of heaven."

Over the centuries, words [especially those of the English language] change in meaning. The word 'humble' is one such word. Humble often being defined as – showing low estimate of one's importance, lowly, modest, of small pretensions. When you look at the full sentence – *'humble himself as this little child'* – I somehow don't feel the child was deliberately and consciously lowering his 'estimate of importance'. Children don't think that way, and that is the whole basis of what Yeshua was saying.

I believe this statement is saying:

Live for the sheer joy of living without thinking how you can become better, greater, or more important than someone else. Live in simplicity. Be playful and creative. Continue to explore your world and your place within it. Allow yourself to trust, be vulnerable, open, and accepting of people for who they are. Learn to stand on your own two feet, to walk, and then to run.

When we strive to be the ego-driven being who needs to compete against others and become 'great' in worldly terms, then we open the pandoras box of tension, disappointments, discontent, jealousy, and resentment. We walk away from the peace and radiance of our true Self – our divinity – our heaven.

REFLECTION

Yeshua was saying, become the 'you' of your divine Self, embrace the innocent child within you, and step into the greatness of the energy within your soul, and then will you enter into the state or 'kingdom' of heaven.

13

THE EYE OF THE NEEDLE

Make the inner journey of release and transformation.

SCRIPTURE

Matthew 19: 23 and 24

23. *"Then said Jesus unto his disciples, Verily I say unto you, That a rich man shall hardly enter into the kingdom of heaven."*

24. *"And again I say unto you, It is easier for a camel to go through the eye of a needle, than for a rich man to enter into the kingdom of God."*

Before we enter into the meaning of these words, let us be clear about the eye of a needle. We are not talking about a sewing needle. Some will dispute me, and that is their right to do so. Either way the message remains the same.

INTERPRETATION

In ancient terms, the eye of a needle described a space that was just large enough for a single man, bent over, to pass through them. For a camel to get through was almost impossible, unless it was an exceedingly small, well trained camel. If a rich man wanted to use that gateway, rather than the main entrance, then one of two things needed to happen.

- If the camel was well trained, then it would have to be unloaded on one side of the wall, the camel would crawl through, and then be reloaded on the other side.
- If the owner of the camel was wealthy enough, he would have two camels - one either side of the wall. The camel carrying the goods would be unloaded, then the goods passed through the gateway to the second camel.

"That a rich man shall hardly enter into the kingdom of heaven."

Note the use of the word 'hardly'. Yeshua did not say wouldn't or couldn't. And heaven in this context does not relate to a place in the cosmos, but to the inner experience of heaven, that state of pure bliss.

The word 'hardly' - of course - comes from hard. Hardly often referring to – with difficulty, scarcely, harshly, in hard manner. So, to put these words of the Master's into context, he was saying that when a person is concentrating on trying to find contentment, worthiness, and happiness by surrounding themselves with worldly wealth and material possessions, they fail to see that true happiness does not come from such things. It is an inner experience with self and the discovery of one's inner beauty and spirituality.

Happiness never comes from our outer world, nor from the love and attention given to us from another. We may know a momentary feeling of satisfaction, contentment, and happiness, but it never lasts. It can't. It fades away as our negative thoughts and feelings return. And what a huge responsibility we place on another's shoulders when we ask of them to 'make' us happy. How can they, when we continue to avoid the inner work we need to do, the work that will help us find true happiness? And how inconsiderate of us to place that responsibility on them. So how do we make ourselves happy?

"It is easier for a camel to go through the eye of a needle, than for a rich man to enter into the kingdom of God."

Let me say that not all wealthy people are miserable or missing the point of how to be happy. I have met wealthy people who are deeply spiritual and absolutely happy. They are usually considerate and giving people. Equally I have met people who are poor that sit in misery and blame everyone else for what has become of them; they are people who have become bitter and hard. Of course, money pays the bills and eases the tension of worry. Of course it is nice to have good quality clothes and the latest of everything. What the prophet is referring to – when material wealth becomes the focal point for happiness, the true path to happiness becomes more difficult to find, not impossible, just difficult. The inner burdens of needing to be loved, needing to feel worthy and worthwhile, wanting to trust others, and longing to be at peace with Self - they become heavy burdens indeed.

So how does the rich man enter into a state of bliss, of heaven within? It is not when his shares rise to bursting point. It is when he takes the burdens off his back, when he offloads the camel, then he can walk through the eye of the needle. To find true happiness is to lift the heavy loads off our hearts and minds; to release the ego-driven human experience of pain, grief, guilt, expectations of others, criticism and judgement of self and others, the bitterness and anger, resentments, and blame. Thankfully, we have a lot of help in our outer world to enable us to take the inner journey of release and transformation.

REFLECTION

One becomes truly wealthy when we open our hearts, not only to the receiving of love, but also to the giving of love. We find heaven within when we become connected to the special and unique energy of our divine soul. It is in the ethereal state of stillness and quiet, of meditation and prayer, we can tap into our own never-ending cycle of peace and happiness – we tap into heaven, the *kingdom of God* that resides in our eternal soul.

14

OF SERVICE

Without the service to humanity, our greatness is lost.

SCRIPTURE

Matthew 20: 26 and 27

26. *"But whosoever will be great among you, let him be your minister;"*

27. *"And whosoever will be chief among you, let him be your servant."*

INTERPREATION

Looking at these two words – minister and servant – my thoughts became increasingly jumbled as I tried to sort out the difference between them. To begin with it seemed simple until I delved a little deeper. In the end I had to bring it to a close, as I got deeper into confusion.

Returning to the Master's words the next day, I was reminded to go back to basics, back to the meaning of servant and minister in Hebrew, which was the prophet's native language.

We also need to be continuously reminded that the Bible has been translated many times through several different languages – Hebrew, Greek, Latin, and finally – English. I can only give my conclusions. As always, seek out what is the truth for yourself.

My understanding now is this:

- Minister – is one who is not attached to any person, but serves others voluntarily from a place of sharing and caring.
- Servant – is one who is attached to a master either by payment or by slavery. They are not free, as a minister would be.

This gives a whole new meaning into the Master's words. Yeshua was asking of them to switch roles. For both of these requests, Yeshua is asking of those with higher roles to let go of ego driven desires for grandeur. So let us examine these sayings a little closer.

"But whosoever will be great among you, let him be your minister;"

Our souls were created in purity and greatness. We all carry the seeds of possibility of greatness within us. Some reach that potential in a lifetime. Others take many lifetimes to let go of fear of failure, or fear of success, to stand in their greatness. But when we do find, and then allow that potential within us to blossom, then the challenge is not to set ourselves above others.

It is our place to then understand that all folks have that potential, and our gifts, achievements, and talents are developed within us to share with or serve our fellow people. In serving others from a place of care and choice, we become a minister to the people. We give of our knowledge, training, and wisdom from a heart-felt place of compassion and care. We ad-minister to them.

We came to this planet of Earth to do two things:

- Learn and grow
- Be of service to others

Without the service to humanity, our greatness is lost.

True equality comes when those who know they are great can begin to see, accept, and nurture the greatness in others, by willingly becoming ministers and sharing what they have discovered within themselves.

"And whosoever will be chief among you, let him be your servant."

And perhaps this is the greater test of the two. What comes to mind immediately as I read these words of the Master are:

- The ever-growing bullying in the workplace, and
- The need for those who are employers to show their superiority over the employee.

In conversation with a woman who has her own housecleaning business, I asked, "Do you have any homeowners who are difficult to work for?" Her reply was, "You would be surprised. I have a couple, held in high regard by the community, who want to treat me like a slave. I don't let them, but they don't like me standing up for myself. I will probably end up losing their business. And then there are those, whom I know really can't afford my services, and they treat me like I am a gift from heaven."

To be a servant is to meet the demands or commands of another from a place of humbleness, and respect. I believe Yeshua is asking of the 'chiefs' to walk a mile in their paid servants' shoes so they may understand how much the servants have given to them; to understand what it means to be respectful of others.

No matter how high a position we may hold – from the head of a household, business, or country – we cannot be there without the servitude of those who are paid to be present for us. When workers go on strike, because those above them are showing no care or respect, everything comes to a grinding halt. Where does that leave the chiefs? No servants, no business.

REFLECTION

It is becoming more evident that those in the upper echelons of power, the chiefs among us, gain more devotion and commitment out of their workers when they allow themselves to show that they understand and have empathy for the lives and working roles of their workers. Those who are servants will work harder for the greater good of all when they are acknowledged for good work done; when they are treated with respect and care.

"And whosoever will be chief among you, let him be your servant." Walk a mile in another man's shoes.

15

THE SHEPHERD

Are you learning to become a shepherd for others?

SCRIPTURE

Mark 6:34

"And Jesus, when he came out, saw many people, and was moved with compassion toward them, because they were as sheep not having a shepherd, and he began to teach them many things."

INTERPRETATION

Shepherds were common before fences were created. They still exist in certain parts of the world, Mongolia for example. What does a shepherd do? He walks with sheep by day, keeping them together, making sure they stay within the boundaries of the farmers acreage, and protects them from the harm of foxes and wolves. Should any wander away, it was the shepherd's place to find them and bring them back into the safety of the flock. He is responsible for the birthing of the young so the flock may keep on expanding. He tends to their injuries, and makes sure they get to water to drink. By night, if there is no yard to herd the sheep into, he sleeps with them, keeping them safe from harm. For those farmers who were fortunate enough to own a flock of sheep, it was the means to their sustenance and income, so the shepherd played an important role in the welfare of the family and community.

Yeshua, observing the crowds of people that came to him, seeing them as flocks of sheep without a shepherd meant:

- They were lost and had strayed away from the deeper spiritual aspect of their selves.
- They were without sustenance and the life-giving water of divine love.
- They were open to being hurt by their experiences without someone to help them heal.
- There was no one to help them give birth to a healthy and abundant life.
- They were at risk of being attacked by the wolves within their societies.

A lot has changed in the last two thousand years. These days more people are moving away from the organised gatherings of the different religions, and are moving more toward their own divine inner journey with self. I am one such person. We prefer to seek out our own truth rather than being told by others what we should or need to believe. The time for others to hold power over us, under the banner of religious law, is quickly dissolving away.

But we are, for the most part, community orientated beings. It is important for us to seek out what is commonly known as 'our tribe'; those people with whom we feel at ease; with, and from whom we can learn.

Growth in any area of our lives needs stimulation. Finding our tribe – our flock - helps us to nurture each other; helps us to give birth to new understandings, new adventures, and the ability to reach deep inside self, discovering our true essence of soul and spirit.

At some stage we all need a shepherd to lovingly guide, teach, and nurture us. Sometimes that shepherd is another human soul, but it can also be a guide in spirit such as Yeshua. I have learned, it matters not what your past religious heritage has been, masters' such as Yeshua and the Buddha are present for everyone. There is no such thing as religions in the vast world of spirit. The realm of masters is a vast one indeed, and made up of many highly evolved souls. They are only interested in being your shepherd, guiding you toward self-love and acceptance, and helping you to evolve into your magnificence as they have done through many lifetimes and experiences.

REFLECTION

'Tribes' may manifest in many ways:

- Walking groups
- Men sheds
- People who meditate together
- Church, temple, or synagogue
- Sports groups
- Nature lovers

Whatever your tribe or your flock looks like, remember you only gain from the group that which you are willing to put into it. Our souls can be nourished in many ways, and our shepherds have many faces. And we are all learning to become a shepherd for others.

16

THE NEED TO BE RIGHT

The need to be right brings about judgement and criticism.

SCRIPTURE

Mark 9: 38 to 40

38. "And John answered him, saying, Master, we saw one casting out devils in they name, and he followeth not us: and we forbade him, because he followeth not us."

39. "But Jesus said, Forbid him not; for there is no man which shall do a miracle in my name, that can lightly speak evil of me."

40. "For he that is not against us is on our part."

INTERPRETATION

Before coming to understand what Yeshua meant by these three verses, there are a couple of things that need to be clarified.

- *Devil* back then was another way of saying mental illness, something which our modern-day medical system is, thankfully, coming to understand. In the Master's time, people who suffered from epilepsy were seen to have a devil in them.
- *Followeth not us* – was not intended as a physical following. It simply means that the person was following a different religion, or a different sect of the Jewish religion.
- *For he that is not against us is on our part* – means that even though he may not belong to our sect, if he is not against what we do and believe, then he is still one with us.

I have never understood why different sects of the same religion need to be at war with each other. As a child, I remember well the division between the Catholics and us Protestants in Christianity. We were encouraged to believe that in some way the other side was different and were not following the religious beliefs correctly. I used to ask my dad, "Why are we against each other Dad, if we all believe in the same Jesus and God? How come the two sides fight each other? Aren't we supposed to love each other?" His answer, "Well if they did it the way we do it, then everything would be okay. You don't understand, and it is too complicated to explain. When you get older, we will talk about it."

We never did talk about 'it' because I began to withdraw from organised religion and find my own form of spirituality. My dad indicated quite strongly that I was a lost soul, and that he was concerned for me. It didn't feel like that to me. Quite the reverse; I began to feel a deepening connection with spirit and a freedom to be who I came here to be without having someone looking over my shoulder, making sure I was doing the right thing by the church.

For a time I threw Yeshua out with the proverbial bathwater until I realised that, in the first place, he never was a Christian and, secondly, he couldn't care less what religion any of us belonged to. There are many roads to the top of the same mountain. He really does not mind which road you want to travel on. It's not about doing what others command of you; it's about going on an inner journey to discover your own deep spiritual Self. At a later time, I reconnected with that master and developed a deep and personal relationship with him that has no link to any religion.

I have listened to my Jewish friends also talking about the different divisions within their faith and how scandalous it is when one group does not follow the strict laws of fundamentalism. That attitude began beyond two thousand years ago. In Yeshua's time it was no different. There were still divisions within the Jewish faith. And so it is within all religious modalities. Why? Because of our need to be right.

Why do we humans have this troublesome need – the need to be right? It has never truly served us. It has created a waring planet, divisions within our personal relationships, and taints our religious journeys; yet it is one of the strongest driving forces within us as individuals, communities, and countries. The need to be right brings about judgement and criticism that is unnecessary. From my observations it comes down to one simple factor – the need to feel safe and in control of who we are, why we are here, and how life will unfold for us. On a daily basis, this is an aspect within me that I am continually watching. I am learning to move away from that need. When the need to be right is no longer present, it is amazing how much you can learn from others, and how much contentment can be present.

In Yeshua's statement - *For he that is not against us is on our part* – is like saying, there is no need to take the stance of 'we are right, and he is wrong' because, in the end, we are all on the same journey however different it may look. Let us look to be unified rather than divided. We are only now beginning to realise how ridiculous it is that sects of the same religion can be at war against each other. Honestly! Do we really think that Great Spirit cares about our petty little differences?

"For there is no man which shall do a miracle in my name, that can lightly speak evil of me."

This statement was made at a time when Yeshua knew that both the leaders of the Jewish community and the Roman leaders were building a case against him with the intent of removing him from the community. He was a rebel and a threat to their power. He was a born leader, and the people were drawn to him as moths are drawn to the flame of a candle. The more I sat with this statement of the prophet, the more I saw into it. Here he is, acknowledging that he is not the only one creating miracles. And he is saying... if this person is creating miracles in the same way I am creating miracles, how could he possibly speak ill of me.

REFLECTION

The Master was healing people by tapping into the Christ energy, the energy he embodied - as we all can. Today we would call it Reiki, or hands on healing. I am trained in Theta Energy healing. The only difference between Reiki and Theta Healing is in the application. My friends who are involved in Reiki healings are working with the Christ energy. As I do Theta Healings, I am working with the Christ energy. The outcome is the same. There is no right or wrong to it – there are only outcomes.

When the Master spoke to his disciples about continuing his work after his death, he told them this, [referring to his work] you will do and more. And they did. And we are still doing it two thousand years later. Miracles happen every day. How could I possibly speak ill of anyone who is creating miracles through Reiki? I do it a bit differently, but we are both using the same source of energy from the magic and power of Great Spirit – the Christ energy!

"For he that is not against us is on our part."

17

WHAT IS SIN?

Peace and harmony in the world begin with peace and harmony within self.

SCRIPTURE

John: 1: 29

"*The next day John* [the Baptist] *seeth Jesus coming unto him, and saith, Behold the Lamb of God, which taketh away the sin of the world.*"

As you may have realised there are two John's:

- John, the author of this gospel, was a disciple and half-brother to Yeshua.
- The John who made the statement in the above verse was John the Baptist.
- John The Baptist was the son of Elizabeth.
- Elizabeth was the cousin of Mary, the mother of Yeshua.

In other words, John the Baptist - who baptised the Master in the river Jordan - was a second cousin to Yeshua.

INTERPRETATION

Behold the Lamb of God, which taketh away the sin of the world.

One could ask, how successful has that been? From my observation it is still pretty prevalent in this world. Again it is all about wording. So let me start with the definition of sin.

There are a myriad definitions of sin.

- A transgression against divine law or morality, especially one consciously committed
- Conduct or state of mind of the habitual or unrepentant sinner
- An offence against any code
- Be ungrateful for one's blessings
- Reprobate, any mortal

The Jewish interpretation of sin is much more simple and complete. Hata [sin] means – to go astray.

From my point of view, one of the greatest sins that has been committed on this planet, is the power play, through centuries, by religious leaders who have [and continue to do so] manipulated peoples' minds and hearts with the threat of punishment, damnation, and hell fire. They preach of sin whilst driving fear into peoples' hearts and demanding obedience to the religion. That to me is sin personified!

John the Baptist, speaking of Yeshua as being the Lamb of God, is a reference to the sacrifice the prophet would make to bring to the world the light of truth for all to hear. Lambs were the animal of sacrifice at that time in the temple. And the Master not only lost his life in order to bring the awareness of the Christ energy to the world, [as they knew the world then], but he also sacrificed his privacy, his home life, and a so many aspects of his life in order to do the work he came here to do. The human Yeshua's life was very much compromised.

And what was that work? *"Which taketh away the sin of the world."* Now we all know that Yeshua cannot just pluck sin away and all will live in peace and harmony. Why? Because we have a thing called free will. We have a choice *to go astray* or to live a life based on love, compassion, and acceptance of each other. So what was John talking about?

To sin is to make a negative choice, to act in a deliberate way that will bring harm to self and to others. Yeshua cannot take that away from humanity. The evidence of that is everywhere. If he could, there would not be freedom of choice, nor would there be wars. What this master and prophet can do, that many other masters since have been doing, is to work with the inner world of people.

Yeshua chose to be present on this planet two thousand years ago to be a teacher and healer, and to show by example how to embody the Christ energy, how to release the power of the negative ego that creates *sin*, and how to embrace the beautiful energy of our divine soul.

REFLECTION

Sin occurs when we forget our divine heritage; forget who we truly are deep within. We are all in this battle of negative thinking, feeling, and doing verses the divine within us. We have all 'gone astray' at some stage in our lives, but we all have the choice that Yeshua showed us – to turn life around and walk in the light of the Christ energy; or to remain sitting in the destructive shadow of the negative ego that creates harm to self and to others.

Peace and harmony in the world begin with peace and harmony within self. We can all embody the Christ energy and *"taketh away the sin of the world."*

18

THE TEMPLE

The heart and its feelings are also the voice of the soul.

SCRIPTURE

John 2: 18 to 21

18. *"Then answered the Jews and said unto him, What sign shewest thou unto us, seeing doest thou these things?"*

19. *" Jesus answered and said unto them, Destroy this temple and in three days I will raise it up."*

20. *"Then said the Jews, Forty and six years was this temple in building, and wilt thou rear it up in three days?"*

21. *"But he spake of the temple of his body."*

As the last line infers, Yeshua was not speaking of a bricks and mortar temple, he was talking about his own body, as the temple which housed his soul. It was a reference to his crucifixion and rising from the dead on the third day. *"In three days I will Raise it up."* The Master knew his time was coming to an end. Imagine living with the knowledge that he was going to suffer one of the worst possible deaths. Yeshua was a prophet of considerable note and, therefore, could see into the future.

INTERPRETATION

I was particularly struck by his reference to his body being a temple. It has been my belief for many years that my body is the temple that houses my soul. Many times I have shared this concept within my workshops and with individual clients.

So let's look at the structure of a temple and see how it aligns with one's body.

- It is made of solid matter – the physical body.
- Usually there are steps leading up to the temple – the seven chakras. The chakras are not a modern-day concept. Ancient Egypt and the Jewish people all believed in the power points and energy centres of the seven main chakras, as did other spiritual beliefs.
- The pillars – which can be seen in the Tarot card of the High Priestess with the letters 'B' and 'J' on them. These symbols first appeared on the pillars at the entrance to King Solomon's temple in ancient Israel. 'B' – Boaz written on a black pillar- stands for completion or endings. 'J' – Jachin [yar-kin] written on a white pillar – stands for beginnings. The release of the old way of being and the beginning of a new way of being. Highly appropriate when seen in the context of Yeshua's resurrection; and in the context of our own journey with life. In addition, pillars are seen to represent strength and stability because they held

the temple up. One could liken the pillars in our temple to our will; the will to stand tall and to achieve what we came here to do. You know that old saying – he is the pillar of the community! He is the strength and the solid foundation on which the community is held up.

- The walls of the temple – protecting the sacredness within – Yeshua's and our souls.
- The domed roof – the skull that protects the vital centre of the conscious, subconscious, and unconscious minds. It also represents the receptive crown chakra that allows the inflow of energy from spirit.
- The Altar – that place from which the life-force flows as the believers come to worship – the heart. The heart and its feelings are also the voice of the soul. Within the soul is found our spirit. The heart has its own wisdom based within love, acceptance, and compassion.
- The Ark – an untouchable cabinet/box which houses the sacred and ancient scrolls of wisdom and knowledge. Only the elected Rabbi, the holy one, is permitted to open that which guards the sacred scrolls. I liken the Ark to our subconscious mind that holds within its core all the wisdom and knowledge gained through many lifetimes. Only we can open the door to our subconscious mind. No one else is permitted entrance.
- The Eternal Flame – which is continuously burning in front of the Ark – the eternal flame of our spirit, our divine self.

REFLECTION

Yeshua was not speaking lightly when he referred to his body as a temple.

It is time to give thanks for the job our body does, to respect it, and to move away from being discontent with our physicality, to loving and honouring our body – the temple of our soul.

FAITH

Have faith in a world we cannot see with the physical eyes.

SCRIPTURE

John 3: 8

"The wind bloweth where it listeth, and though hearest the sound thereof, but canst not tell whence it cometh, and wither it goeth: so is every one that is born of the spirit."

INTERPRETATION

There have been many times in my journey where I have been tested by other people, and by what I see and hear from spirit. But this saying of Yeshua's is one I have used many times to bring myself back into faith with the beautiful beings with whom I am privileged to communicate. It is also one I have used with my more scientifically minded friends who find my trust in a realm of spirit to be misguided and fantasy.

As the Master said, we cannot see the wind, but we know it exists. We hear it, and we see the evidence of its presence through the movement of leaves and what we feel. When I use this analogy, my friends always come back with, "But we can tell you how the movement of air that we call wind is created." To which I reply, "Yes. That is your training. But if you had not been trained in science, would you still know that the wind exists? My training for a very long time has been in psychic ability and being a medium for spirit. I came into that training because – like you did with the wind – I felt the presence of spirit and saw the evidence of its existence."

"So is every one that is born of the spirit."

We are all born of spirit. Every tiny babe comes into this world with a soul that houses their spirit. We hear daily references to the spirit within and are asleep to the meanings of the words. He is a high-spirited person. She is in low spirits. But is this what the Master was talking about?

I think Yeshua was actually referring to the spirit realm. At the time he was talking with a Jewish ruler called Nicodemus [who, by the way, referred to Yeshua as Rabbi, inferring that he was highly trained in the Jewish tradition and had earned the right to be a Rabbi].

In verse 6 of the same chapter Yeshua says, *"That which is born of the flesh is flesh; and that which is born of the spirit is spirit"*. Put differently; those who are born with a solid body are easily seen - because they have a body. Those who are born of [or into] spirit do not have a physical form and therefore, (like the wind, and like thought), exist, but we only know of their existence because of what we feel, or evidence of their existence through other means. As the wind ruffles the leaves of trees to announce its presence, so too do those who are in spirit, find ways to allow us to know they are with us.

The wind is like thought. Where do our thoughts come from? How are they created? We all know we have a brain, but how is thought produced within that brain? No scientist yet has been able to tell us how we think. They can tell us from what part of the brain it is created, but no-one knows just how we formulate thought. Yet each of us has thousands of thoughts in a day, most of which we are unaware. We believe in thought. We believe in the presence of wind. Why then is it so hard to believe in the reality of a spirit realm? Thought is very much of spirit. Through mental telepathy all mediums hear the thoughts of spirit beings. Energy – like the movement of wind – is very much of spirit.

REFLECTION

Because we are three dimensional beings, it is hard for us to believe, and have faith in a world we cannot see with the physical eyes. "Show me the evidence," say my scientific friends; to which I reply, "Show me the evidence of thought." Thought is all around us from other people. Thought is within us all of the time. But we cannot see it nor do we know from whence it comes. And so it is with beings we cannot see from our three-dimensional perspective. We are all born with psychic abilities, and more people every day are awakening to those abilities. In doing so, the doors are creaking open to the realm of spirit. It is no longer uncommon to be a medium. There are thousands of us all around the world. Through these courageous people, the reality of the realm of spirit is being proven and made clear. We are now reaching a point where scientists can no longer ignore the voices of many. Some scientists are beginning to realise that we are not the only people inhabiting this cosmos... and some of us don't have a need for a physical body.

"The wind bloweth where it listeth, and though hearest the sound thereof, but canst not tell whence it cometh, and wither it goeth: so is every one that is born of the spirit."

20

THE LIGHT

Where light shines darkness cannot exist.

SCRIPTURE

John 3: 20 and 21

20. *"For everyone that doeth evil hateth the light, neither cometh to the light, lest his deed should be reproved."*

21. *"But he that doeth truth cometh to the light, that his deed may be made manifest, that they are wrought in God."*

What of this word – evil? Often defined as bad, harmful, malicious, believed to do material harm, slanderous

In the Bible evil takes on a different definitions:

1. profoundly immoral and wicked:
"his evil deeds" - *"no man is so evil as to be beyond redemption"*
2. profound immorality and wickedness, especially when regarded as a supernatural force: *"his struggle against the forces of evil"*

INTERPRETATION

It is foolish to deny the existence of such harmful forces in our world. One only has to look at the history of war on our planet for thousands of years to understand that evil exists. However, it is a word I use with great care. From my experience with the realm of spirit, I have never encountered evil in the seventy years I have been in contact with other beings. I am not saying it does not exist. We can't be the only waring planet in all of the cosmos. What I am saying is, I have never encountered it. Why? Because where light shines darkness cannot exist. And that is exactly what Yeshua was saying.

When I am describing to people in workshops how powerful light is, I use the following analogy:

Place in your pocket a box of matches and a candle. Walk into a room that has no window and is completely painted in black – walls, ceiling, floor. Close the door and take a few steps into the centre of the room. You will immediately feel disorientated. Fear begins to touch your mind. Where is the way out? I am starting to feel claustrophobic! Now take out the box of matches and light one. Even with that tiny light the darkness begins to disappear, and fear begins to lessen. Now pull out your candle and light it. The darkness cannot exist where there is light. You can now find your way to the door and out into the brighter light of day.

"For everyone that doeth evil hateth the light, neither cometh to the light, lest his deed should be reproved."

Those whose intent is to be harmful to others are coming from a place of needing to be in control, and are using the negative energy of the ego. We have all had a touch of that at some stage with the use of damaging words or action, through being hurt, jealous, or feeling inferior. In this mind, they are usually standing in the self-righteous power of the mind with little compassion coming from the heart. When in that self-righteous place, the last thing they want is to have someone shine a light on what they have done, and who they were in that moment. To be reproved, is to be blamed, accused of being guilty, rejected for what one has done, and judged for what has taken place.

In John 11: verse 10, Yeshua also said, *"But if a man walk in the night, he stumbeleth, because there is no light in him."*

REFLECTION

"But he that doeth truth cometh to the light, that his deed may be made manifest, that they are wrought in God."

When we stand in the truth of our soul, our divine spirit, we stand in the light of divine grace and love, both from within us and from the beautiful ones in spirit who walk beside us, those magical beings of light. From within that place of our divinity, our sacred soul space, we are capable of creating whatever journey in life we desire.

The word 'wrought' means to be worked into shape or form, to be artistically created, fashioned in a specific way, or – as is the case with metal, to be hammered or beaten into a desired shape. In other words, with the help of our guides in spirit [God], we can shape [wrought] our lives in a creative way that will bring happiness and fulfilment, providing we are creating it from the divine truth within us. We allow ourselves to also become beings of light and love.

21

THE WELL

The awakening to the realisation that we are all divine.

SCRIPTURE

John 4: 13 to 15

13. " *Jesus answered and said unto her, Whosoever drinketh of this water shall thirst again,*"

14. " *But whosoever drinketh of the water that I shall give him shall never thirst; but the water that I shall give him shall be in him a well of water springing up into everlasting life.*"

15. " *The woman saith unto him, Sir, give me this water, that I thirst not, neither come hither to draw.*"

INTERPRETATION

In this story of the prophet, Yeshua and his disciples had been walking on the road from Jerusalem, through Samaria, on the way to Galilee. There was, [and still is], a well in a town called Sychar. This was Jacobs well. Sychar is a place of history and no longer exists except for fragments of buildings that still stand. The closest place now to Jacob's well is Nablus. Nablus is a town forty-nine kilometres north of Jerusalem, situated on the west bank of the river Jordan. It was Samarian country. The Samarians and Jews had little to do with each other at that time.

The disciples went on ahead of Yeshua to get food whilst he remained at the well to drink. A Samarian woman came to the well to draw water to take back to her household. The well was deep. Yeshua found it difficult to reach down to where the water was, so he requested the help of the Samarian woman, asking her to draw up some water for him to drink. The woman was amazed that he would speak to her and ask for her help.

"Jesus answered and said unto her, Whosoever drinketh of this water shall thirst again,

But whosoever drinketh of the water that I shall give him shall never thirst."

The Master was, of course, not talking about physical water when speaking of the gift he would bring to all humans. The gift of water that he was referring to was the wisdom, knowledge and the awakening to the realisation that we too are divine, and have within us the well of our own spirit housed in our soul. Once again, the embodiment of the Christ energy - he came to teach, and show us how to access that well of divinity that lies deep within us.

Being dissatisfied with life - that kind of thirst, without the deeper love for self and acceptance of self, is insatiable. When we become aware of the peace, stillness, and loving power of our divine spirit within, and draw from that well our strength and courage, we will go on to live a happy and contented life. We will know a *'well of water springing up into everlasting life'*.

"The woman saith unto him, Sir, give me this water, that I thirst not, neither come hither to draw."

The woman didn't get what the Master was trying to say to her. She was still thinking of the precious water she was taking back to her family. She was saying – if you give me of this water, I will never have to come to this well to draw water again. Have you ever tried carrying a big bucket of water? It is heavy work, especially when you have to carry enough to keep a whole family going. Who can blame her for not understanding what he was saying? In this account of his interaction with the Samarian, Yeshua didn't go on to explain himself.

It is difficult to fully grasp the significance of that well of divine water within us. Our spirit within our soul is another side of us, and is elusive. In our daily work of making sure we are fed, clothed, have the bills paid, and meeting with our needs for life, means we often forget the most important aspect of our existence. Yet, when we tap into that deep inner well, we are unstoppable.

Many years ago, I answered a call in the early hours of morning to a woman who pleaded with me to come to her house and pick up herself and her son. She and her husband had a massive argument. Physical violence was a possible outcome. Both had been drinking alcohol. Both were equally to blame for what had occurred. When I arrived at the house, their son of eight years was standing between them with his arms outstretched, one towards his mother and one towards his father – holding them off. He had said to them, "If this doesn't stop, I will call the police."

This child was a karate student. Travelling back to my place, he was sitting in the front with me; his mother quietly crying in the backseat. I said to him, "You were the adult in that situation. Where did you get the strength to do what you did?" I will never forget his response, nor the actions that went with it. He said, "My karate Sensei, [teacher] told us to go inside and draw from our deep well of strength and courage." As he spoke, he cupped his hands, from out in front he drew his hands into his abdomen, then he pulled the energy upwards from his abdomen to his chest. I remember thinking as I drove home, there are a couple of people tonight who could learn from their eight-year-old son.

REFLECTION

The child instinctively knew that to stop the violence from escalating, he had to go deep to the source of his power and call forth what was required to prevent his parents from harming each other. He was aware the power existed because, with the simple acceptance of a child, he took on board what his Sensei had told him. In that moment the power came to him. In those crucial minutes, he prevented a disaster because he believed in his inner power. That power came from the deep and endless well of his divine spirit.

Yeshua is one of many Sensei's. The realm of masters is full of them - teachers of profound wisdom and knowledge.

"But the water that I shall give him shall be in him a well of water springing up into everlasting life."

22

THE DEAD SHALL HEAR

Listen to the inner voice of your divine soul for it has great wisdom.

SCRIPTURE

John 5: 24 and 25

24. "Verily, verily, I say unto you, He that heareth my word, and believeth on him that sent me, hath everlasting life, and shall not come into condemnation; but is passed from death unto life."

25. "Verily, verily, I say unto you, The hour is coming, and now is, when the dead shall hear the voice of the son of God; and they that hear shall live."

What is the meaning of verily? It must be significant for the Master to have used it four times within such a short piece of speech. It means - truthfully, truly, honestly, certainly. So another way of saying *verily, verily I say unto you* is to say truthfully, certainly I will tell you…

Yeshua was talking to his fellow Jewish people in the temple on their holy day. On such a day no work was to be done. In the fundamental Jewish culture the same applies to this day. But this recalcitrant Rabbi chose to heal a blind man on their sabbath day and therefore went against the ruling. At this stage, because of his popularity amongst the people, the leaders of the Jewish community were looking for ways to bring him down. In these two verses, by healing a blind man, Yeshua was trying to get across to his people that there are greater things at play than disobeying the rules of the temple. So what was the message he was trying to convey to them?

"He that heareth my word, and believeth on him that sent me, hath everlasting life, and shall not come into condemnation; but is passed from death unto life."

The soul is eternal. We never die except to the physical self. That is what is meant by *'passed from death into life'*. In other words, death is a transition from this lifetime back into spirit. What did the Master mean by – *'and shall not come into condemnation?'*

INTERPRETATION

I do not believe for one moment that he was talking about us being condemned by himself or a god. I believe he was talking about self-condemnation. If I were to rewrite this sentence of Yeshua's, here is what I would say:

If you listen to what I am saying, and believe in a great spirit, which is a part of you and you are a part of it, then you will come to understand your own journey with your soul and you will step out of condemning yourself. Instead of dying inwardly with self-judgement, you will reclaim a beautiful life and live it to the fullest. And you will come to understand that physical death is a portal through which we all pass back into the realm of spirit.

"Verily, verily, I say unto you, The hour is coming, and now is, when the dead shall hear the voice of the son of God; and they that hear shall live."

One might ask, how can the dead hear someone's voice?

Let me work this sentence in a different way:

Honestly, surely, what I am saying to you is this – the time has come for people, who feel dead inside themselves, to listen to what I am conveying to them. We never die. We make a transition from one life to another. And those who receive my message will regain a sense of their eternal soul. They will begin to truly live and not just exist.

Aside from the message the Master was conveying, let me address my thoughts on doing nothing on the holy day. It was the same in my father and mother's Christian home. We only did the bare essentials on a Sunday, the day we went to church. For my Jewish friends, it is a Saturday. It was considered a day to rest and to contemplate one's life. In some ways, as a society, we are missing out on the blessings of this mindset. There are benefits to be gained in having one day in the week where you place your concentration on the inner journey rather than rushing around. Each year, my husband and I take a week - separately - to be alone and to meditate, contemplate our future, and concentrate on our inner journey with self. We go on our individual retreats. It is a precious time to re-evaluate who we are and our place in this world. The busyness of life can swallow us up, leaving us stressed and out of touch with our true essence – the magic of our spirit.

REFLECTION

Take time out to be with I, me, and myself; to listen to the inner voice of your divine soul for it has great wisdom. Begin to truly live and not just exist. To just exist is to die to Self. To live is to embrace all of who you truly are.

23

EASTER

Love is the greatest conqueror of all.

SCRIPTURE

John 7: 1 and 6 and 7

1. *"After these things Jesus walked in Galilee; for he would not walk in Jewry, because the Jews sought to kill him."*

6. *"Then Jesus said unto them, My time is not yet come; but your time is always ready."*

7. *"The world cannot hate you; but me it hateth, because I testify of it, that the works thereof are evil."*

I write on what is known as Easter Friday, or Good Friday. On this day, Christians honour the crucifixion of Yeshua by the Jews. On the same day the Jewish community celebrate the eve of Pesach. Most people know it as the Passover. Pesach goes back a very long way to when Moses leads his people out of Egypt, thus ending their slavery to the Egyptians. I find it an interesting observation that the new religion of Christianity, born out of the Jewish faith, chose the Jewish day of celebration of freedom to honour the death of their Master at the hands of the Jewish people.

INTERPRETATION

Remembering that Yeshua was a prophet, he knew long before the movement against him began that he would die at the hands of the leaders of the Jewish community. He knew he was a threat to their power. He knew his rebellious nature, his desire to bring to the people a different way of thinking was going to land him in trouble. The same people who had been released from the bondage of slavery in Egypt, they were the very same rulers who were restricting the lives of people with the threat of death if they did not adhere to the rules and regulations of fundamental Judaism. *For he would not walk in Jewry,* [meaning the area in which the Jews lived and ruled], *because the Jews sought to kill him.* It was the Pharisees – the political Jews – who were the ones to ultimately bring about Yeshua's death.

Will we never learn on this planet? Those who have had an injustice done against them, they then become the perpetrators of injustice. And so societies for centuries have swung from one to the other. Why is it so difficult for people of Earth to grab hold of the notion that love is the greatest conqueror of all? Yeshua knew it, and tried to convey that message to the people of all backgrounds.

"The world cannot hate you; but me it hateth, because I testify of it, that the works thereof are evil."

Remembering the meaning of words have changed in the past two thousand years; evil back then meant to be mentally unstable, hungering for power, and therefore to do harm from that place. As we look at the wars that are still going on, the same struggle for power exists as it did then. Both the Jewish and Roman leaders of that day truly hated Yeshua because he brought attention to the different communities of how corrupt their leaders were.

How fortunate am I to live in a country where freedom of speech, and the ability to be equal to any man, is a preserved right of our nation. Even today, as it was back in the Master's time, there are still religious societies where freedom of speech is greatly restricted. If these societies were truly spiritual, then such restrictions would not apply. Herein lies the difference between religion and spirituality.

Religion has its base within humanity. Spirituality has its base in the love of Great Spirit. Religion applies the rules and regulations of a human race, a race that struggles between the ego of the mind, the need to have power and control over its adherents, and the love of the heart. Spirituality is based on the journey of the soul and its connection to all of life within the cosmos; a connection that says I am one with all that exists, and all that exists is one with me. The soul cannot know hatred. It is in the mind and the power of the ego that hatred exists.

As I sat quietly, deep in meditation this morning, I sought to understand why Yeshua was such a threat to the Jews at that time. Why did they need to kill him in such a brutal way? Why the need to try and crush him by making him suffer the worst penalty – to die a horrendous death among murderers and thieves? Such was their fear of being exposed for their corruption; and their fear of losing control of the people. And the same fears still exist on this waring planet of Earth.

The irony of what the Jews did to bring about the Master's demise – instead of bringing him down, they made him a hero and brought about the creation of a new religion. What they were trying to stamp out is the very thing they ultimately created. Yeshua brought love and healing to the people. The people saw that the Jews brought anger and violence to Yeshua. Is it surprising then that people began to see the difference? Since that time, there have been many atrocities created in the name of Christianity. The past two thousand years have not exactly created a good reputation for this offshoot of the Jewish community. Where the ego and its need for power resides, there you will find people lost to their deeper journey with the soul.

REFLECTION

Only respect for each other, acceptance of our uniqueness and individuality, acknowledging the right of each person to be who they came here to be, and tapping into the source of light and love that lies within our gorgeous souls – only that can bring an end to the destructive journey of the ego that Yeshua spoke about two thousand years ago.

24

TRUTH

Taste the deliciousness that comes with freedom, the richness of being true to you.

SCRIPTURE

John 8: 31 and 32

31. " Then said Jesus to those Jews which believed on him, if ye continue in my word, then are ye my disciples indeed."

32. "And ye shall know the truth, and the truth shall make you free."

What did the Master mean – *'if ye continue in my word?'* Perhaps a different way of saying this would be – if you continue to do what I say, to believe in the truth as I see it, to walk a different path to the one you have been told you must tread – *'then are ye my disciples indeed'*. Note he did not say followers. He used the word disciples. So what is a disciple? A disciple is a student. In the Oxford dictionary, the word discipline which is associated with disciple means:

Training – especially of the kind that produces self-control, orderliness, obedience, and capacity for co-operation.

The difference between a follower and a disciple is this:

- A follower idolises someone and wants to be in their presence. They admire what the person does, says, and stands for, but may not be all that serious about making changes in their lives.
- A disciple is a student who has the self-discipline and desire to learn from a teacher and leader, who is prepared to make changes in their lives according to what they learn, and will strive to become as good as the teacher.

To this day Yeshua still has followers and many disciples.

"And ye shall know the truth, and the truth shall make you free."

Gandhi, another master who came to teach peace and freedom, and was shot for his efforts, said that 'they' could imprison his body, but not his mind. This was the exact same message that the Master conveyed to his disciples just hours before he was crucified. No one can take your truth from you. It resides deep within you. And Nelson Mandela said, "As I walked out the door toward the gate that led to my freedom, I knew if I didn't leave my bitterness and hatred behind, I'd still be in prison."

INTERPRETATION

Truth and freedom go hand in hand. There are two types of freedom – freedom of the physical and freedom of the inner Self. These three great masters were all speaking about the inner freedom.

The soul and its spirit are eternal. The only one who can imprison one's mind, and heart is Self. That kind of imprisonment comes about through negative thinking and feeling. But no-one can imprison the soul. For a time the physical body acts as a carriage, if you like - a car - and enables the soul to be present in this physical world of Earth. When death brings an end to 'the cars' journey, the soul opens the door and climbs out, returning back to the realm of spirit. It cannot be imprisoned.

When you stand in truth; when you see what is right for you; when you let go of expectations from and toward others; and when you begin to live your life from within you, from your source of light and love, rather than seeking the approval of the outer world - then you begin to taste the deliciousness that comes with freedom, the richness of being true to you.

I remember well a moment with my son when he was nearing the end of his secondary education and was laying down plans for his university training. One evening he came to me and said that he was confused about what direction he should take. My son was a person who operated equally from the left and right sides of his brain. He was both a scientist and a musician. Members of the family were trying to encourage him to do a degree in medicine, or law, or science research – working from the left side of his brain. But his passion was in music – right brain activity. At that time he was playing drums and percussion with five different music groups. I asked him what was confusing him. He replied, "I don't know if I should apply to do a science degree or an arts degree majoring in music." I asked him to close his eyes. As he thought about doing science how did he FEEL. He said he felt heavy, burdened, a bit scared. When I asked him to note how he felt with the thought of doing an arts degree in music, he replied he felt excited and warm. I then said, "You have your answer. You will do music. That is where your heart is at. That is your truth." He went on to become a lecturer in music at two universities in Melbourne, Australia. Several years later he went on to do a PhD, which had elements in it of the science of music. He has often said how fortunate he was to be living his dream and to be working at something he loves. My son listened to his truth and found freedom within his inner music.

Truth is a massive word. What does it mean to be true to self?

- Listen to the voice of your heart – your feelings. The mind and its thoughts can bring you into confusion, but your feelings never lie.
- Give up trying to live up to the expectations others' have of you. Live to your expectations of Self.
- Stop being a slave in pleasing others at the expense of denying your own precious journey. Of course, it is a beautiful thing to be present for others and to do things for them that bring them pleasure and joy. But when you do it to gain their admiration and favour – then you become imprisoned by the need to be accepted and noticed.
- Discover what is your truth in your spiritual journey. Always there will be those who want you to walk their path. Often, they believe it is the only path. There never is only one path to the top of the same mountain. Walk the path that is right for you. There is no right or wrong, there are only differences.

REFLECTION

We are all here, every single individual across this planet, to learn one simple lesson - how to live a joyful and free life from within us; to discover that the source of lasting happiness can never be found in the outer world; and to embrace our power as a unique, loving, and compassionate soul.

That is the truth that sets us free.

25

GODS

Our ego pushes us to depths that force us to seek the peace and stillness of the god within.

SCRIPTURE

John 10: 30 to 34

30. "*I and my Father are one.*"

31. "*Then the Jews took up stones again to stone him.*"

32. "*Jesus answered them, Many good works have I shewed you from my Father; for which of those works do ye stone me?*"

33. "*The Jews answered him, saying, For a good work we stone thee not; but for blasphemy; and because thou, being a man, makest thyself God.*"

34. "*Jesus answered them, Is it not written in your law, I said, Ye are gods?*"

INTERPRETATION

If, as I do, you interpret Father as being Great Spirit, then this saying of the Master's makes total sense – "*I and my Father are one*"'. We are all one with Great Spirit and Great Spirit is one with us – in us, around, above, and below us. There is no separation. Yeshua was not excluding others from being one with that intangible force; he was simply using his awareness, his life as an example of what can be achieved. It was difficult then, as it is today, to help people to comprehend we are more than flesh and blood. We are also spirit and eternally linked into that force I call Great Spirit. Humanity has been so focused on the outer world, and our place within it, it is difficult to take time to go inwards on a journey of self-discovery of our divinity. But whether we are aware of it or not, we are all interlinked into that massive energy field.

"Then the Jews took up stones again to stone him."

Note the word – again. Twice the Jews took up stones with the intent to stone Yeshua. The first time was when he healed a blind man on the sacred day. It is a part of his history we don't get to hear much about. The attempt at stoning came within a short time before his crucifixion, and was part of the political endeavour to turn the people against him.

"For a good work we stone thee not; but for blasphemy; and because thou, being a man, makest thyself God."

Yeshua was not in the process of making himself into a god. He already was God. Because of the strict rules around religion, the power play by those in high places, and the need to stop a rebellion against the Jewish rulers - for a man to claim he was already God was a big threat. To be a beacon of light, leading people away from those who had power over them into finding their own inner divinity, to become God within, created a lot of fear in the minds and hearts of those rulers of the Jewish community who were revelling in their ego driven power. And Yeshua's reply to them says it all.

"Jesus answered them, Is it not written in your law, I said, Ye are gods?"

For most people, it has taken a couple of thousand years to come to terms with this idea [and many still cannot accept] that within them is a divine spirit – for that is what a god is, a divine spirit. The 'I' in this statement – I said, Ye are gods – is reference to the being who channelled the laws to the Jews that they hold sacred.

In my role as a psychic medium, I have often heard criticism about the 'New Age' concept. The idea of us being gods and goddesses is often called 'airy fairy stuff'. Yet, here we are two thousand years ago with Yeshua reminding the Jewish rulers that in their sacred scriptures they are referred to as gods.

Let me just say there is nothing new about the New Age. Most of what is practiced has been around long before Yeshua appeared. What is new about it is the right for people to believe and practise whatever spiritual path they feel is perfect for them. It is only in the past twenty years I have felt the freedom and the acceptance from others for me to be true to who I am. That is new! Prior to that, many wonderful spiritual psychic people were considered mentally unstable. For the past two thousand years - be you Jew, Christian, or any other religion - people were held in the power play of those who set themselves up to be the conscience of the community. The history of the Christian hierarchy has been, at times, anything but loving and caring. There has been much brutality performed under the guise of Christian ethics.

REFLECTION

We are gods. We are part of and one with Great Spirit. *"I and my Father are one."* But we are also human. Housed within this human form are two aspects that seem to be in a constant tug of war with each other – our divine spirit [god] and our ego.

Divine spirit of the soul, and ego of the mind. It is when we learn to hush the chatter of the ego through meditation or prayer, we come into the peace and stillness that allows us to go deeper within and discover our god-self, our divine heritage of spirit.

Once the god within becomes a reality for us, the power of the ego lessens. It never goes away. It can't and shouldn't. Our ego is a fabulous teacher showing us what not to do, and pushes us to depths that force us to then seek out the peace and stillness of the god within. *I said, Ye are gods!*

HOME OF SPIRIT

We will all return to our soul families – old or new.

SCRIPTURE

John 14: 2 and 3

2. " In my Father's house are many mansions: if it were not so I would have told you. I go to prepare a place for you."

3. "And if I go and prepare a place for you, I will come again and receive you unto myself; that where I am, there ye may be also."

Deceased author, Dr Michael Newton, left us a legacy of invaluable books - *Journey of Souls* and *Destiny of Souls*. These books were written after he had worked with thousands of clients, recording what he found under hypnosis - as Dr Brian Weiss has done. Michael was a high-profile psychiatrist, like Brian, who was deeply respected for his research into life beyond the grave. In these books, he wrote of these 'mansions' within spirit. Each of us has a soul family. As a general rule, each one within that soul family are progressing in spiritual growth at roughly the same level of excellence.

Every now and then a member of that soul family may decide to progress faster in their growth. They will choose to reincarnate into a life that will push them to their limits, helping to accelerate their personal growth. When this happens, and they pass through the death process again, rather than returning to their previous soul family, they more than likely will seek out a new soul home that is equal to the growth they have made. I recommend reading these books if you are seeking a deeper awareness of what life in spirit is really like.

INTERPRETATION

Yeshua was addressing his disciples when he made the statement, *"I go to prepare a place for you"*. He was letting his disciples know that his time to die was approaching; that he was going to return to his home in spirit, and once there, he would make sure that all was in order for his disciples when their time to leave their bodies, and return back to spirit, had arrived. Note: the Master did not say you will be coming to my soul family. Rather, he said… *"I go to prepare a place for you"*. My feeling about these words: the disciples [because of what they had learned from being with Yeshua] were not going to return to their old soul families; that their growth had accelerated and, therefore, they would return to a different soul family, one whom the Master would prepare for the return of the disciples, as they pass through the veil between this life and the next.

"I will come again and receive you unto myself."

As one who has worked with people moving through death - as a nurse, a counsellor, and a psychic medium – on many occasions I heard the one dying say that a loved one, who had already passed, was with them. On a few occasions I have heard a dying person say that Jesus was with them, or some other highly evolved deity, and that they had come to escort them home. It is not a new occurrence. For centuries those who have passed through death have been escorted home by loved ones.

What Yeshua was saying to his disciples was this: when your time to die and return back to spirit comes, I will come to you, and I will hold you and escort you back to your soul family. You will see me again.

REFLECTION

As a nineteen-year-old nurse, into my third year of training, I was privileged to be present when a six-year-old girl in our children's ward was dying of a brain tumour. She had been in a deep coma for some days. I was on a late evening shift. Her parents had been summoned when it was becoming evident that she was letting go of life. As her parents stood by her bed, she suddenly opened her eyes, looked at her parents, and said, "Don't worry Mummy. Don't worry Daddy. Jesus is here with me. He is lovely. I am safe." She closed her eyes, and died. Deep as their grief was, those last words their daughter spoke brought them a moment of peace.

"That where I am, there ye may be also."

And Yeshua continues to escort people back to their home in spirit. We will all return to our soul families – old or new. We may not be in his particular *'mansion'*, but we will be in his country. We will be Home!

27

I AM THE WAY

Live by my example and you will find your way to heaven within.

SCRIPTURE

John 14: 5 and 6

5." *Thomas said unto him, Lord, we know not whither thou goest; and how can we know the way?"*

6. *"Jesus saith unto him, I am the way, the truth, and the life: no man cometh unto the Father, but by me".*

INTERPRETATION

I am quite certain that Yeshua was not saying, as most Christians believe, that he was the only portal through which one could pass into heaven beyond death.

The Jews have always believed that they were the chosen ones. The doctrine of Christians, as a result of these few words – '*no man cometh unto the Father, but by me*' – have adopted a similar attitude; one that says unless you become a Christian you will be refused entry into heaven. To exclude all other people on this planet, who live by a different faith, from the state of divine bliss and entry into heaven is both a form of control over the people and arrogance.

When one looks at the history of the Jews and Christians, neither have set a good example to the rest of the world in showing the way to heavenly bliss. The persecution and killings by the Christian church during the medieval part of our history undertook crimes equal to what Yeshua went through in his crucifixion, and perhaps worse. One would doubt that the Master would have looked on favourably to such a horrendous force of control and power over the people in his name. And remembering it was the Jewish leaders who hung Yeshua on the cross, their actions say the same thing – unless you adhere to our way of being, and follow our rules, you will be stoned or hung on a cross.

Thomas' question of the Master – *"how can we know the way?"'* - was answered with – *"I am the way, the truth, and the life"*. Put another way:

If you live by my example, then you will find your way to heaven within. I am showing you the truth of the existence of your divinity by embracing who I truly am, a divine being of light and love. At your very core, that is who you are, eternal souls that hold within your soul's energy the connection to Source, Great Spirit, God, The Father. That is the truth, and that is the life – eternal life.

God and Father is the magnificent force for which there cannot be any human comprehension or understanding. It is not, and never has been a single being. It is a force far greater than our capacity and ability to wrap our thinking around. Yeshua knew beings of the human race needed to have a way of connecting with such a magnificent force, as people still do today. As souls we all come from the source of that power, hence 'Source' becomes Father [or God], from which our souls were created/born. Our modern-day word 'Source', to describe that energy, was equivalent to Yeshua's use of the word 'Father' or 'our creator'. Whenever the Master spoke of his heavenly Father, Yeshua was putting Source into a framework that his disciples could understand. From that energy our souls were born, and to that energy we will ultimately return. We are one with and part of God or Source. God, (or Source), is one with and part of us. When we incarnate into physical form as a human being, we forget from whence we have come, but we always return to our home - back to Source.

"No man cometh unto the Father, but by me."

As said before - the Bible has been translated many times before arriving at the King James version. Two thousand years of shifting languages can change the original meaning of Yeshua's message.

Working as a medium, communicating with many souls in spirit, and working extensively with this beautiful soul on behalf of others, I am certain within myself that the prophet did not mean he was the only one through which human beings could access Heaven. When one considers how long life has existed upon this planet, and how many religions existed before Christianity was created, it is ridiculous to believe all those people would be denied entry into heaven. Equally ridiculous is the notion that Christians are the only ones who hold the only key into the heavenly realms.

So what was meant by those words? I believe, Yeshua was saying that if you follow my example and take the inner journey of discovering your connection to the Father, (Source), within your soul's energy, then like me, you will discover the door that opens the way to both heaven within self in this lifetime, and heaven beyond death.

The Master did not arrive at his place of divine connection without a lot of hard work, study, and travel to many parts of his then known world. To obtain his bar mitzvah at the age of twelve, Yeshua had to study the Jewish scriptures thoroughly. He went on to become a Rabbi, which meant further study. He sought out the wisdom of elders from many areas of the world. He went on a journey of self-exploration, study, meditation, and prayer. He came to terms with both his human Self and his divine Self. He learned how to become a healer and a prophet. He was charismatic and a born teacher. Yeshua was devoted and dedicated to becoming a shining example to people, to show them the 'way' to becoming magnificent beings of love and light, as he was.

REFLECTION

It is when we step into this journey, we discover our own magnificence. We also discover that heaven is not only a place in spirit, but a state of being that draws us into the power and love of Source, the Father, that incredible energy beyond human comprehension.

28

MANIFESTATIONS

Only through connecting to our heart and soul can we manifest miracles.

SCRIPTURE

John 14: 10 to 12

10. "Believest thou not that I am in the Father, and the Father in me? The words that I speak unto you I speak not of myself: but the Father that dwelleth in me, he doeth the works."

11. "Believe me that I am in the Father, and the Father in me: or else believe in me for the very works' sake."

12. "Verily, verily I say unto you, He that believeth on me, the works that I do shall he do also; and greater works than these shall he do; because I go unto my Father."

INTERPRETATION

"The words that I speak unto you I speak not of myself: but the Father that dwelleth in me, he doeth the works."

I facilitate workshops on psychic abilities. One of the aspects of working with our psychic abilities that I am adamant about, especially when we begin to use them in helping other people, is to always remember we are conduits through which our soul and Great Spirit work. This is exactly the message Yeshua was conveying to his disciple Phillip. Phillip had said to the Master, *"Lord, shew us the Father, and it sufficeth us."* And Yeshua had asked, don't you believe that I am in the Father and the Father is in me? As discussed in the previous chapter, and placing this statement of Yeshua's in a more modern context, another way of saying this would be:

"Phillip, don't you believe that I am one with Great Spirit, and that Great Spirit is in me and works through me? You have known me all this time, and still you have not got comprehended this. The Father is not a physical or singular being; the Father is Source that exists within our soul-self."

When we deliberately work with our psychic abilities and our gifts as a connection between the world of humanity and spirit, as mediums, we need to make sure we are not sitting in the energy of our ego-self, of our humanness. The moment we lose sight of why we are being a channel, and for whom we are being a channel, we can potentially damage peoples' lives.

When we begin to believe our voice is more important than the voice of spirit, we lose the power of connection to spirit. Our guides will step back and say, "Over to you. If you think you know better than us, and the messages we have been bringing through you, then let us see what the outcome will be." You know that old saying that pride comes before a fall. There is a truth in those words. When the ego of the mind takes over, and we forget that we are only the conduit, that we are part of a team of spirit beings, then what follows is usually a lesson, often via another human being, in the importance of working with our soul's loving energy and not the energy of our mind.

"Believe me that I am in the Father, and the Father in me: or else believe in me for the very works' sake."

Yeshua performed many miracles with the disciples present. Yet still they found it hard to comprehend how the Master accomplished such things. These words the Master spoke are like saying – if you can't believe in the concept of me embodying the Christ energy, the divine spirit, then at least take a look at what has been accomplished through the work I have done, and see the magic of what has been created.

"He that believeth on me, the works that I do shall he do also; and greater works than these shall he do."

In other words:

If you embody the Christ energy, opening your heart and mind to working as one with spirit, then you can do what I have been doing. And not only will you do what I have been doing, but you will do even greater works than what I have.

Can you imagine that? How incredibly amazing that would be. And yet it is happening every day - we just don't see it. So many people have cured their illnesses by working with the energy of the soul and with Great Spirit.

Thousands of people around the world are helping people to heal mentally, emotionally, and physically. Physical illness is often a reflection of mental or emotional problems. When you heal the mental and emotional issues, the physical can follow suit. When you add the power of healing from the Christ energy – miracles happen. But miracles don't happen from the head space. Only through the connection to the heart and soul can we manifest miracles. One has to have the faith that what we want to manifest can truly be done. It is through meditation, [in any of its many forms], and through prayer that we can reach deep into our inner being, reach deep into Source, and create from that divine place.

"Because I go unto my Father."

Yeshua was telling his disciples the time had come for them to take over. He knew his death was not far off. Being the prophet he was, the Master knew that the Jewish leaders were becoming agitated with what he was saying. In voicing these messages to his disciples and his followers, Yeshua was taking the power away from the Jewish leaders, both political and religious, and placing that power where it belonged, within their own selves.

REFLECTION

And that is where it still belongs. Not within the hands of any leader of any religious sect, but within our own divine inner journey with our soul. Within our soul we each have the power to interconnect with Great Spirit and the energy of the cosmos. Within our soul we have what it takes to do what Yeshua did – and more.

This power within us is called The Source, The Christ energy! When we know its power, we can truly create our own heaven on earth!

THE JOURNEY

Journey beyond the safety of your comfort zone and discover the essence of who you truly are.

Creating Heaven on Earth has taken me on an amazing journey; one of healing and discovery. As I near the end of writing these chapters, I am aware that any number of people could have written this book; people who are more qualified in the study of the scriptures. I feel humbled and deeply privileged to have been the author. I sit with a strange combination of feeling sad, knowing the completion is in sight, and excitement for its future. I am beginning to feel an emptiness as I let go of the book. In a strange way, it has become its own entity. I will miss sitting in the energy of the divine Master. We have walked a path of renewal and intimacy with each other. But it is done, and the time has come to let go and move on to another creation.

My connection to the Master and prophet, Yeshua- whom I once rejected because of my own father's Christian voice – has strengthened. It has strengthened because I found the courage to look beyond the pain of childhood, to reach beyond the dogma, and to allow a new understanding to find its way into my mind and heart.

You may agree or disagree with what has been written. Neither concerns me, so long as you have allowed yourself to open up to a new way of thinking and being. Always reach for the greater you, your soul-self. What others believe to be right for them may not necessarily be right for you. You do not need to reject it all, as I did, but rather take from the many spiritual teachings, from all walks of life, and find your own deep, intimate, and personal truth.

Looking back over this journey with Creating Heaven on Earth, I have realised:

- My dad's presence has grown stronger, and a bond has been created between us that was never present when he was here on earth. I now know, I chose my own earth father so I would be challenged by his Christian dogma, that I may see the difference between religion and spirituality. Such a precious gift he gave me.
- There has been a build-up effect from chapter to chapter that I was unaware of happening during the writing.
- The human Jesus was just as important as the divine soul. Like all of us, he needed to know his humanity to recognise his divinity.
- The Bible only gives us a tiny, framed portion of the Master's life. There is much more that the old scrolls are only now revealing. And even they tell us little of his journey between his bar mitzva, at the age of twelve years, and when he returned to the people in his thirties.
- After all of these two thousand plus years, we still struggle with the concept of peace, forgiveness, and

unconditional love. Still we sit with anger, resentment, and violence.

My wish for you as you read this book:

Honour your physical body for it is the vehicle in which your soul can be present in this world. Love who you are, all of you, for there is no other like you; no other who can think and feel as you do. Whatever negative thoughts you have about yourself, become the alchemist, and change the negative into the positive. Create what is right for you, not what others may wish for you. Become the master of your life. Journey beyond the safety of your comfort zone and discover the essence of who you truly are. Yeshua did – and so can you.

Beyond the barriers of religious belief, may you discover the beautiful connection between this master – and all masters – and your journey within this human existence. Remember, there are no religious divisions in the realm of spirit, for we are all one. And to know we are part of a never-ending cycle from birth through death and back to birth again. In truth, there is no death, only the continued learning for the soul until we return home to Source – to the Father. In the words of the Master... *Ye are Gods!*

PRAISE FOR JOY BRISBANE

Robyn Sedgwick
Masters of Spirituality from the University of Divinity

Bravo Joy!

Firstly, it is a brave thing to offer a response to Biblical quotes through a personal lens and channelled understanding. This is not a work of academic theology but rather a generous sharing of one woman's journey to liberation from the shackles her father's fundamentalist interpretations of Christian teachings, religion, and spirituality.

Joy has forged her own authentic spiritual pathway. It is wonderful to read her reframing of old teachings into new interpretations that support her on that pathway. She is a medium and psychic who values and trusts her channelled communications. She writes confidently of her own connection to and perception of Jesus or Yeshua much more in keeping with a loving God/Universe/Source.

This book encourages others who are seeking to find their own truths, to try a new lens especially those who have had to wrestle with religious frameworks that have sold them up the river.

Some formal religions fail to stand up to the scrutiny of lived human experience. Joy has answered back and forged her own authentic spiritual pathway. She is courageous and unafraid of any reverberations she may encounter. The key take away for me was:

"We are all here - every single individual across this planet - we are here to learn one simple lesson: how to live a joyful and free life from within us; to discover that the source of lasting happiness could never be found in the outer world, and to embrace our power as a unique loving and compassionate soul."

That is the truth that sets us free. Creating Heaven on Earth shares her reframing of old teachings into interpretations that have supported her on that pathway. As a medium and psychic, Joy values and trusts her channelled communication. Her own connection to, and perception of Jesus [or Yeshua] reflects a loving God or Source beyond the constructs of any one religion. It is more aligned with the generosity and loving approach found in A Course in Miracles.

Joy offers her unique perception of spirit, truth, and the non-physical realms in a way that challenges old understandings. At the very least, she invites the reader to reconsider their own spiritual or religious beliefs, and to look deeper at their own belief systems.

Faye Spurr – division one nurse

The interpretations of the gospels have made me joyous. Joy in the empowerment of unconditional love. The explanations and re-definitions of the meanings of words allow the gospels to come into the modern world. This really resonated with me as the traditional interpretations of the gospels did not make sense.

I have found the bible difficult as it appears to have many conflicting examples about love, judgement, and ego. This interpretation of the messages is aligned with my beliefs and now I am looking at these passages with a new perspective. This book has made me think more deeply about the messages and their true meaning, but also has prompted me to really examine how I think and pray.

I feel relieved that the bible can be interpreted with such a pure message of love.

Jan Smith – holistic healer

Thank you so much for allowing me to read your new book. I absolutely loved it. It resonated with me on so many levels. As you know I work with and channel the energy of Jeshu on a daily basis and have felt that since reading your book that my healings have gone up another level and his energy is coming through stronger and clearer. I have felt more motivated and have a stronger sense of purpose since reading your wonderful wisdom. It helped me to understand his teachings on an easier level.

Belinda Fyffe CEO – The Proven Group

I read this book *hungrily* as I have only done twice before, once with Eckhart Tolle's *A New Earth*, and with Neale Donald Walsh's *Conversations with God*. I found myself enthralled with Joy's book as with few others. Having had a very Christian upbringing, and now not practicing any religion, I found this fresh take on some of the most well-known bible phrases to be invigorating and refreshing. I found myself feeling that I was having the words of a wise man unpacked so that they made sense to me in the 21st Century, in a way they never had before. The words of any wise person are designed to point the way to assist us to a deeper understanding and appreciation of our human journey – this book certainly assists with that.

Allan Meers – chartered accountant

For me, Creating Heaven on Earth presents a fresh view of the words of Jesus. I found it interesting that, while the views presented are not from a traditional Christian perspective, they resonate strongly with understandings found in many other spiritual traditions of which I am aware. I believe, Joy Brisbane's book provides insights rarely found in biblical literature. It provides a way forward for people to come together in a spirit of harmony, each seeing the power of Jesus' words in ways that touch both head and heart. As such, it deserves to be discussed widely by people of many faiths - or no faith – and create a forum for new ways of looking at what spirituality means in the 21st Century.

ALSO BY JOY BRISBANE

From the Contemporary Interpretations of Scripture Series Joy Brisbane bring us...

Illumination - Walking into the Light of Love

NOTES

NOTES

www.ingramcontent.com/pod-product-compliance
Lightning Source LLC
Chambersburg PA
CBHW062038290426
44109CB00026B/2663